Fascism
and
Communism

European Horizons

Fascism
and
Communism

François Furet and Ernst Nolte

Translated by
KATHERINE GOLSAN

With a preface by
TZVETAN TODOROV

University of Nebraska Press
Lincoln and London

Original title: *Fascisme et communisme*
© For the Ernst Nolte Letters, François Furet–Ernst Nolte,
Feindliche Nähe 1998 by F. A. Herbig Verlagsbuchhandlung
GmbH, München. © Librairie Plon, 1998.

Preface and translation © 2001 by the
University of Nebraska Press
Manufactured in the United States of America

∞

First Nebraska paperback printing: 2004

Library of Congress Cataloging-in-Publication Data
Furet, François, 1927–
[Fascisme et communisme. English]
Fascism and communism / François Furet
and Ernst Nolte; translated by Katherine
Golsan; with a preface by Tzvetan Todorov.
p. cm.—(European horizons)
Translation of: Fascisme et communisme.
Includes bibliographical references (p.).
ISBN 0-8032-1995-4 (cloth: alk. paper)
1. Fascism. 2. Communism. I. Nolte,
Ernst, 1923– II. Title. III. Series.
JC481 .F88 2001
335.43—dc21   00-054514

ISBN 0-8032-6914-5 (paper: alk. paper)

Contents

Preface to the English Edition

Tzvetan Todorov

Translated by Mary Byrd Kelly

In the present little volume, one can read a confrontation between two preeminent historians on one of the most serious subjects of our time, the history and meaning of the attack on liberal democracy by fascism and communism. The two authors debate their interpretations after having written extensively on the subject: Ernst Nolte (born in 1923), in a whole series of works centered on the evolution of European fascisms; and François Furet (1927–1997), an authority on the French Revolution, in his last book, *Le Passé d'une illusion* (1995; *The Passing of an Illusion,* 1999), devoted to the history of the communist ideal in the twentieth century. Finished just days before Furet's death, our small book can be considered his spiritual testament, and it constitutes one of Nolte's last important stands.

In reading this book, we are witnesses to something so rare that it demands our attention: a true dialogue.

Not a superficial exchange of polite words, nor the rhetorical competitiveness that can be observed in a public oral debate on the speaker's platform at a colloquium or in front of television cameras, nor a scathing polemic due to the rivalry between two specialists. No, in this instance the two authors treat each other first and foremost with mutual respect, at the same time acknowledging that they disagree. Each then tries to change the other's mind, or at least to make more sense out of their disagreement. Neither author seeks to come across as the winner, to dazzle the audience with some brilliant turn of phrase. Instead, they both try, with the help of rational arguments, to come a bit closer to historical truth and to moral or political justice.

Out of respect both for these two authors and for the readers of the present volume, who, I presume, are capable of forming their own judgments in the debate that takes shape in this book, I will refrain from pronouncing my own opinions here. I have neither more knowledge nor more wisdom than François Furet and Ernst Nolte, especially when they come together. I will therefore content myself with giving a reader's impressions concerning the meaning and the stakes of the debate.

We must first pinpoint what the two authors' positions have in common, even beyond their ability to examine any question without worrying beforehand about the political correctness of their remarks. Above all, it is their desire to examine fascism and communism at the same time. The reason for this combination is twofold: the similarity and the interrelationship of the regimes. The two movements represented parallel attacks on liberal democracy, which is what a generic term like "totalitarianism" implies. At the same time, they were in a state of constant interaction for as long as fascism lasted, opposing each other, secretly competing with each other, actively collaborating, and finally battling each other in all-out war.

This rapprochement between the two antidemocratic regimes was prevalent in the historical and political debate of the 1930s, but a permanent reshuffling ensued with Germany's invasion of the USSR and the establishment of an alliance between the Soviet Union and the Western democracies, the United States and Great Britain. The three allies could henceforth be grouped together under the common label of antifascism, a strange combination of democracies and their enemies. After the war, when no one yet knew the extent of communist crimes, the revelation of the scope of Nazi crimes made comparing the two regimes awkward for many people. It was perceived as a purely polemical argument, one forged for the needs of the Cold War. It would not be until dissidence mounted in the Soviet Union and Eastern Europe, and then the communist regimes collapsed, that the question could be reconsidered not in a political context but in a specifically historical one.

To be more precise, the similarity and interrelationship of the two regimes gave birth to two different approaches. The first established a typology of political regimes, and it naturally found its place in works of philosophy or political science, the authors of the best-known of these being Hannah Arendt, Carl Friedrich, and Raymond Aron. The second approach, a historical one, questioned the chain of events itself; Nolte was one of its pioneers, and Furet chooses to follow him along this path. Both authors thus eschew the "structural" approach in favor of "genealogical"

analysis, although it would perhaps be more helpful to
see these two approaches as complementary, not rival.
Analysis requires a knowledge of facts and events as much
as it demands rigor in the concepts used.

Rapprochement does not mean identity or equivalence,
and comparison of the regimes reveals similarities and
differences alike. On this point, Furet and Nolte agree
too, just as they do in attributing exceptional status to the
destruction of the Jews under the Third Reich. This status
is not due to the number of victims. In 1932–1933, Stalin
deliberately brought death by starvation and deprivation
to six million peasants in the Ukraine, Southern Russia,
and Kazakhstan, a figure similar to the number of Jews
put to death by Hitler. What sets the Holocaust apart is
this crime's place in overall Nazi politics: putting people
to death became an end, not a means. There was no Tre-
blinka in the communist system. What came closest to it
were the systematic exterminations of the elite of certain
"enemy" nations, as in the case of twenty-two thousand
Polish officers in 1940; but such facts remain marginal in
communism, whereas they are central for the Nazis. In
Soviet camps, death was not a goal but either a punishment and means of terror, or else an insignificant loss and
accident. Death took on no particular meaning there; life
simply no longer had any value.

Finally, Furet and Nolte both seem to say that the liberal and democratic system constituted what Furet calls
"the matrix of the two great ideologies, communist and
fascist," which only took the contradictions inherent in
this matrix and pushed them to the extreme. Precisely
because the authors agree with each other, they do not

seek arguments in support of their thesis, when in fact it could use a few. Must one hold liberal and democratic thought responsible for all of modernity's vices? Is the modern age as homogeneous as this genealogy would have us believe, and can its ideological core be identified simply by turning to the now distant Enlightenment?

It is within this common framework that disagreements between Furet and Nolte appear. Some of them are purely verbal and are cleared up in the course of discussion. Others are real but devoid of historical interest. Thus Nolte shows an inexplicable curiosity for "negationist" writings, as if they had not already been refuted some time ago.[1] Certainly every historical question is legitimate, but some answers are both false and pernicious. Therefore, they are not worthy of the historian's attention, and they deserve instead not legal condemnation, it is true, but scorn and silence. There nevertheless remain two basic questions raised by the debate, one concerning the causal link between Bolshevism and fascism, and the other relative to the rationality of human actions.

Since they both place themselves in the "genealogical" perspective, Furet and Nolte must specify the nature of the ties between rival antidemocratic movements. Nolte emphasizes succession (Bolshevism preceded fascism) and gives it the role of a causal nexus: fascism was born in response to Bolshevism, as a defensive reaction. Furet, on the other hand, sees the two phenomena as parallel, having a common source: the critical assessment of liberal democracy and bourgeois individualism. Neither author denies the presence of elements favoring the adverse thesis, but they give them a position that sometimes prevails and at other times does not. My personal impression as a reader is that Furet's arguments are more convincing than Nolte's.

The second question concerns the Nazi extermination of the Jews and could be put this way: Can one say that Hitler's conduct was rational? This question immediately brings up another, preliminary one: What do we mean by the rationality of an action? The difficulty in answering this question stems perhaps from the fact that we attach a certain prestige to reason and therefore have trouble acknowledging that actions that we consider heinous can arise out of some sort of rationality. We would prefer that these actions be the doings of demons and devils, or at least of delirious madmen, not of ordinary human beings. In this way, we raise a barrier between them and us, and we do not feel too threatened by their "paranoia" or their "insanity." Benjamin Constant, at the turn of the nineteenth century, was much more pessimistic in this regard when he remarked, "In the name of infallible reason, Christians were thrown to the lions and Jews were sent to the stake." Postulating the irrationality of evil is often a reaction of self-defense and an easy way out.

The distinction between "rational" and "irrational" actions is probably not applicable here. There are reasons for every action, even the most blameworthy: reason is easy to bend at will, ready to become the instrument for achieving any end. This does not mean that everything in history can be explained, but that reason must not be rejected as a tool of analysis (on this point Furet ends up coming around to Nolte's position). However, the rationale for any action may either be shared by everyone or not. The essential distinction would thus be between actions whose rationality is purely subjective (existing solely in the individual subject's perspective) or intersubjective, that is to say, capable of being rightly accepted by the subject's contemporaries or by historians of a later day. Only this second form of rationality can be transformed into legitimacy. Hitler's deductions were not irrational from his own point of view. They sprang from incontestable observations, like the large proportion of Jews in the initial leadership of the Bolshevik Party, but they do not lend themselves to being shared by others, for they go against the moral intuitions characteristic of the human species.

The debate between Nolte and Furet raises questions that concern us all, and not only those keenly interested in the history of the twentieth century, for the writing of history is not just an attempt to grasp the meaning of events and get closer to the truth. Through the choices and constructs that it compels us to make, it also brings into play our conception of what is just and what is good.

Foreword

In the summer of 1996, François Furet wanted to publish his correspondence with the famous German historian Ernst Nolte in *Commentaire*. Its appearance in Italy sparked a debate that stirred as much interest in France as in Germany.

The debate arose out of a footnote in Furet's last book, *Le Passé d'une illusion*,[1] devoted to the interpretation of fascism proposed by Nolte. In January 1996, Ferdinando Adornato, editor-in-chief of the journal *Liberal* in Rome, took the initiative of asking Nolte to respond to Furet's analysis. Nolte did so in the form of a letter to which Furet replied in turn. Eight letters were exchanged in this manner, and they comprise the current essay on the twentieth century, communism, and fascism.

In May 1997 François Furet obtained Ernst Nolte's permission to prepare a French edition. He made a final revision of his text, and during a trip to Aix Island, Napoleon's last stopping place in France, we agreed on the form this publication would take.

Then the terrible news arrived. François Furet had died in Toulouse on July 11, 1997.

Thus, it was after his death that this correspondence appeared in *Commentaire* (nos. 79 and 80, fall 1997 and winter 1997–1998). The correspondence testifies to François Furet's reflection on our historical destiny because it is an analysis of the entire twentieth century, an extension of his final book stimulated by the encounter and debate with a German historian and philosopher who himself devoted his work to a major question for Europe: the seeds of communism and fascism.

The French edition of this translation reproduces the letters of François Furet and Ernst Nolte as they appeared in *Commentaire*. Those of Ernst Nolte were translated from the German by Marc de Launay. It was revised by the author and the editorial staff of *Commentaire*.

The correspondence between the two historians ends with François Furet's lines, placed in epigraph to this volume as a tribute to his memory. They express with a Tocquevillian sadness his feelings at the end of his life and describe Europe's situation at the end of the twentieth century.

The editors of *Commentaire*

> *Such is the melancholy backdrop of this century's end. Here we are enclosed in a single horizon of history, pulled toward the standardization of the world and the alienation of the individual from the economy, condemned to slow the effects without having a hold on their causes. History appears all the more sovereign as we lose the illusion of governing it. But as always, the historian must react against what seems inevitable at the time he writes; he knows too well that these kinds of collective givens are ephemeral. The forces that work toward the universalization of the world are*

so powerful that they trigger sequences of events and situations incompatible with the idea of the laws of history, a fortiori *of possible prediction. Understanding and explaining the past is already difficult enough.*

FRANÇOIS FURET

Fascism
and
Communism

1

On Ernst Nolte's
Interpretation of Fascism

François Furet

The war of 1914 has had the same seminal character for the history of the twentieth century as the French Revolution did for the nineteenth.[1] The events and movements at the origin of the three "tyrannies" that Élie Halévy spoke of in 1936 issue directly from it. Chronology says as much, since Lenin took power in 1917, Mussolini in 1922, and Hitler failed to do so in 1923 only to succeed ten years later. This suggests a temporal affinity among passions ignited by these novel regimes that made the political mobilization of former soldiers the means of total domination by one party.

This perspective opens another avenue to the historian for the comparison of dictatorships of the twentieth century. It is no longer a question of examining them in light of a concept, at the moment when they respectively reached the height of their curve, but rather of following their formation and successes, so as to grasp what is specific to each one and what they have in common with one another.

What the history of each one owes to relations of imitation or hostility maintained with the other regimes from which it borrowed certain traits remains to be understood. For that matter, imitation and hostility are not incompatible; Mussolini borrows from Lenin, but only to vanquish and forbid communism in Italy. Hitler and Stalin will offer many examples of belligerent complicity.

This approach, which constitutes a natural preamble to an inventory of a category such as "totalitarianism," has the advantage of more closely following the movement of events, but it runs the risk of offering a simplistic interpretation through linear causality. Thus, the Mussolinian fascism of 1919 can be seen as a "reaction" to the threat of Italian-style Bolshevism, also arising out of the war and following more or less the Russian example—a reaction in the broadest sense of the word, since Mussolini, who, like Lenin, comes from an ultrarevolutionary socialism, can more easily imitate it in order to fight it.[2] Also, the victory of Russian Bolshevism in October 1917 can be made the point of departure for a chain "reaction" by which Italian fascism first, Nazism later, appear as responses to the communist threat, modeled on the revolutionary and dictatorial mode of communism. This type of interpretation can lead, if not to a justification, at least to a partial exoneration of Nazism, as the recent debate on the subject among German historians has shown: even Ernst Nolte, one of the most profound specialists on fascist movements, has not always escaped this temptation.[3]

For twenty years, but particularly since the 1987 debate, which made German historians grapple with the subject of the interpretation of fascism (*Historikerstreit*, 1987), the thought of Ernst Nolte has been the object of

such a perfunctory condemnation that it warrants particular comment.

One of his contributions is early on to have gone beyond
the ban on drawing parallels between communism and
fascism, which was a more or less general prohibition
in Western Europe, especially in France and Italy, and
particularly absolute in Germany, for obvious reasons,
which still persist. As early as 1963 in his book on fascism
(*Der Faschismus in seiner Epoche*; *Three Faces of Fascism*), Nolte advanced the broad outlines of his historico-
philosophical interpretation of the twentieth century, at
once neo-Hegelian and Heideggerian. The liberal system
(by what it offers as contradictory and at the same time
indefinitely open to the future) constituted the matrix of
the two great ideologies, communism and fascism. Marx
opened the way to the first, which takes the "transcendence" of modern society to the extreme, by which the
author means the abstract idea of democratic universalism, which wrests human thought and action from the
limits of nature and tradition. In the opposing direction,
fascism seeks to protect men from the anguish of being free and open-ended. It draws a remote inspiration
from Nietzsche in its will to protect "life" and "culture"
against "transcendence."

Thus, one cannot study the two ideologies separately:
together they lay out, in a radical fashion, the contradictions of liberalism, and their complementarity-rivalry
has filled our entire century. But they are also inscribed
in chronological order: the victory of Lenin preceded the
victory of Mussolini, to say nothing of that of Hitler. In
Nolte's eyes, the first event affects the two later ones, and
he never ceases to develop this relationship in later books

(*Die Faschistischen Bewegungen*, 1966; *Deutschland und der Kalte Krieg*, 1974; and above all *Der Europäische Bürgerkrieg, 1917–1945*, 1987). On the ideological level, the universalist extremism of Bolshevism provokes the extremism of the particular in Nazism. On the practical level, Lenin's extermination of the bourgeoisie in the name of the abstract idea of a classless society creates a social panic in the part of Europe most vulnerable to the communist threat and prepares the way for the triumph of Hitler and the Nazi counterterror.

However, Hitler himself fights a losing battle against his enemies; he too is caught in the universal movement of "technique" and uses the same methods as the adversary. Like Stalin, he stokes the fires of industrialization. He claims to defeat Judeo-Bolshevism, this two-headed monster of social "transcendence," but he wants to unite humanity under the domination of the Germanic "race." Thus in this programmed war, nothing will remain of the reasons for winning it. As Nazism proceeds, it betrays its original logic. It is again in these terms that Nolte, in one of his recent works (*Martin Heidegger, Politik und Geschichte im Leben und Denken*, 1992), explains and justifies his former mentor's brief militant period, which favored Nazism. For Nolte, Heidegger was right to be at once enthusiastic and quickly disappointed by National Socialism.

It is understandable how and why Nolte's books shocked the postwar generations. The latter were confined by guilt, or by a fear of weakening the hatred of fascism in trying to understand it, or simply by the conformity of the period. At least the reasons for the first two reactions are noble; historians can and must respect them.

But if they were to imitate them, they would not allow themselves to take the Soviet terror into consideration as one of the fundamental elements that contributed to the popularity of fascism and Nazism in the twenties and thirties. They would have to overlook what the arrival of Hitler owes to the precedence of a Bolshevik victory, the negative example of pure violence erected as a system of government by Lenin, and finally the Kominternian obsession with spreading the communist revolution to Germany. In reality, the refusal to recognize these considerations prevents the elaboration of a true history of fascism. In the historical domain, this refusal is the counterpart of the Soviet version of antifascism in the political domain. In forbidding the critique of communism, this type of historiographic antifascism also prevents an understanding of fascism. Breaking this taboo is one of Nolte's primary contributions.

What is unfortunate is that he weakened the impact of his interpretation on the discussion of Nazism among German historians by exaggerating his thesis; he tried to make the Jews, as allies of Hitler's enemies, into Hitler's organized adversaries. Not that Nolte is a "negationist."[4] On many occasions he has expressed his horror of the Nazi extermination of the Jews, and even pointed out the uniqueness of the Jewish genocide as an industrial liquidation of a race. He supports the idea that the Bolshevik suppression of the bourgeois as a class paved the way for the Holocaust, and that the gulag precedes Auschwitz. But the Jewish genocide, if it is in line with the tendency of the period, is not only a means to victory in his eyes; it has the special horror of being an end in itself, a product of victory, of which the "Final Solution" was the main objective. In attempting to explain Hitler's anti-Semitic paranoia in a recent article, Nolte appeared to find a kind of "rational" foundation in a declaration of Chaïm Weizmann in September 1939 in the name of the World Jewish Conference (*Historikerstreit,* 1987), asking Jews all over the world to fight on the side of England. The argument is both shocking and false.

Clearly the argument is part of a strain of humiliated German nationalism of which Nolte's adversaries have accused him for twenty years and which constitutes one of the existential underpinnings of his books. But even if this is partially true, the accusation cannot discredit a work and an interpretation that are among the most profound this last half-century has produced.[5]

2

Beyond Ideological Impasses

Ernst Nolte

MY DEAR COLLEAGUE,

I would like to share some more personal and less detailed thoughts on your book, *Le Passé d'une illusion*, than those in my essay published at the request of Pierre Nora in *Le Débat*.[1]

It has been almost a year since I first got wind of your book through an article in the *Frankfurter Allgemeine Zeitung*, which not only emphasized its importance but expressly made mention of the long note on pages 195–96 referring to my own works. Thus, no doubt I was aware of it sooner than I would have been in ordinary circumstances, and I read it, line by line, with the greatest interest and with aesthetic pleasure as well.

I quickly realized that your work was free of two impasses or two obstacles that in Germany confine all reflection on the twentieth century to a narrow space and that, in spite of all the laudable individual efforts, render it impotent. In Germany, this reflection, in fact and in principle, has attached itself completely and almost exclusively

to National Socialism, and because its catastrophic conse-
quences are obvious, too often formulas have replaced the
work of thought—formulas such as "delirious ideas," "the
singular German path," or "a criminal people."

There were clearly two perspectives of thought that
went beyond the German limits, but one, the theory of
totalitarianism, was considered obsolete by all the "pro-
gressives" by the middle of the 1960s, or even appeared to
be an instrument of the Cold War. The other, the Marxist
theory, was seldom developed in enough depth to show
the Third Reich as a simple part of a much larger, and
for this reason, guiltier whole—Western imperialism, for
example, or the world capitalist economy.

The German and French Left

The German Left did not have a single perspective on its
own history because this history itself was not simple.
There was no big event with which it could identify itself without reserve, because even the wars of liberation
against Napoleonic France were not without what were
perceived to be "reactionary" motives, and the revolution
of 1848 had been a "failure." Only a small fraction of the
German Left identified itself with the Russian Revolution,
and Social Democracy, by far the largest and most important part of the German Left, was resolutely opposed, in
theory and in practice, to an extension of this revolution
to Germany. Certainly, if it were possible to measure the
enthusiasm and intensity of faith that this revolution inspired inside the Left, more than half of it would have
to be attributed to the German communist party, because

the Social Democrats fought the communists with what could only be called a "bad socialist conscience" and the KPD [Communist Party of Germany] was the only party in Germany whose importance grew significantly in elections, even in the November 1932 vote when the National Socialists were roundly defeated. But even among the young neo-Marxists of the 1970s, very few would have retrospectively considered a communist victory believable at the turning point of 1932–1933 or would have accused the Social Democrats of "betrayal." It is precisely this opinion, but with an opposite slant, that constituted the "right-wing" anticommunist thesis that one couldn't accept *post festum* either, that is, that communism reflected a real danger and that it was *for this reason* that National Socialism acquired so much power. But even in the eyes of the big parties of "Weimarian democracy" reconstructed in Bonn after 1945, this idea could only appear erroneous and dangerous because it offered too many analogies with the National Socialist thesis, which claimed to "save Germany from Bolshevism," and because, in an alliance with the United States, these parties had committed themselves to driving back the attacks of "totalitarian Stalinism" and its German representatives in East Berlin.

The theory of totalitarianism certainly provided a way out in offering a distinction between "democratic" anticommunism and "totalitarian" anticommunism, but it did not prevail for long, and following this, from Right to Left, from press to university, all spokespersons agreed to concentrate on the examination of National Socialism and to focus on "Stalinism" only in passing, without speaking of a "world communist movement" at all. These are the two "impasses" I referred to.

You, however, start from the "communist ideal" in your book, and you see it as the most powerful ideological reality of the century. You don't confine it to the limits of Russia, where a pragmatic foreign policy prevailed very quickly, and you speak of "the universal charm of October," which sparked the enthusiasm of numerous intellectuals, above all in France. You can do this because you come from the French Left, which, contrary to its German counterpart, has access to a great event in its national history to which it can untiringly lay claim—the French Revolution—and through which it was able to consider the Russian Revolution as a consequence and a counterpart, a revolution for which it could, in good conscience, feel sympathy, without always enthusiastically identifying with it.[2]

Also, it was not by chance that a large majority of the Socialist Party at the 1920 Congress of Tours claimed allegiance to the Third International, that famous historians of the French Revolution such as Aulard and Mathiez sympathized with the world movement and even became members.[3] But other personalities as well whom you mention, men such as Pierre Pascal, Boris Souvarine, or Georg Lukács, were enthusiastic and convinced, and you yourself clearly were interested in and sympathized with this enthusiasm. Of course, little by little historical reality sapped the faith of a Pierre Pascal, of a Boris Souvarine, as of so many others, and you also followed these dissidents; but in spite of the separation, you continue to see in the Russian Revolution of October and in its world extension the fundamental political event of the twentieth century.[4] You pursue the examination of its extension until, exhausted by its struggles with multiple realities, it loses its internal force and at last ends up being what it was from the beginning because of its utopian character: an "illusion."

But you take another step that is no less decisive in my eyes. If the fundamental event of the twentieth century reveals itself finally to be an illusion, the militant reactions it provoked cannot be placed beyond all understanding nor be totally void of historical legitimacy. The fact of refusing to perceive "otherwise than as a crime the other power of fascination of the century" must also be considered an unjustified residue of the communist vision. This assessment of "the other great myth of the century," that is, the fascist myth, has encountered much opposition, even in France, whereas in Germany today, you risk quickly becoming a "person to be avoided."

However, in my opinion, you are absolutely right that no one can reasonably suspect you of thinking that the fight between the communist idea and the opposing fascist idea is the *sole* content of the history of the century between 1917 and 1989–1990, or that fascism should be considered a kind of platonic idea, without taking into account the multiple differences and presuppositions that determine all historical reality and, therefore, also the reality of the world communist movement.

By a completely different path from yours, I managed to surmount these two "impasses" and thereby develop the idea (long since outlined) of the ideological civil war of the twentieth century. I also would have gone no further than an exclusive interest in National Socialism and its "German roots" if I had not discovered by chance that the socialist thought of the young Mussolini was influenced as much by Nietzsche as by Marx. For this reason alone,

"fascism" could become a subject for me in my 1963 book;
and the general definition of fascism as a militant form of
anti-Marxism, as well as the specific definition of National
Socialism as "radical fascism," already contained virtually
everything that I have since been able to think and write.
But the "communist idea," which, for you, was the point
of departure, remained, for me, at most a backdrop that
wasn't really explicit, and it was only in 1983, with my
book *Marxismus und industrielle Revolution*, and above
all in 1987 with *Der Europäische Bürgerkrieg, 1917–1945*,
that things changed.

The Genetico-Historical
Version of Totalitarianism

If I am not mistaken, from distinct points of departure
and taking different paths, we both arrived at this idea
that I call the "historico-genetic version of the theory
of totalitarianism," which distinguishes itself almost as
much from the politico-logico-structural version of Hannah Arendt and Carl J. Friedrich as from the Marxist-
communist theory.

However, it seems that there is a profound point of
divergence between us. In the note I referred to, you write
that it is sad that I exaggerate my interpretation and that
I have given "a kind of rational foundation" to "Hitler's
anti-Semitic paranoia." I certainly don't need to stress to
you that the singular event of massive destruction triggered by the "Final Solution of the Jewish question" fur-
nished important justifications for the fact that German
historical research has concentrated on National Social-

ism. And from your perspective, certainly you will agree with me that in History what is singular cannot pass for an "absolute" nor be treated as such. I would add: a unique mass crime is no less horrifying or worthy of condemnation if it can be given a rational intelligible grounding; quite the opposite. May I remind you that in one of your 1978 articles, you criticized the French Left's simplistic interpretation of Zionism, and you wrote that the nature of this phenomenon could not be isolated from Jewish messianism?[5] You didn't use quotes, so therefore considered the term legitimate even though obviously you know as well as I that it is possible to speak of a "Russian" or "Shiite" messianism. I think that the "Final Solution" cannot be intelligible *[verstehbar]*—as opposed to understandable *[verständlich]*—without having recourse to "Jewish messianism," as such, and to the idea that Adolf Hitler and a good number of his followers had of it. For this reason I think it is possible to resolve the difference that separates us. Be that as it may, and to use an expression cited many times by the German writer of French origin, Theodor Fontane, this is a "vast terrain." To cultivate this terrain in an appropriate manner will require many words and thoughts.

It is to be expected that in Germany, if I claim that the success of your book delights me as much as it does you, my comments will serve to denigrate you, even to incriminate you; but I believe that in your country the prejudices and hysteria are less powerful than in mine.

Sincerely yours,
ERNST NOLTE

Berlin, February 20, 1996

3

A Taboo Subject

François Furet

My Dear Colleague,

I knew very well that I would unleash hostile feelings toward my book in your country and even beyond when I devoted this long footnote to you. It didn't fail to do so, since just the fact of citing you triggers near "Pavlovian" reactions on the Left; Anglo-Saxon historians as different as Eric Hobsbawm and Tony Judt criticized me for simply citing your name, without feeling the need to justify this excommunication. The spell of this banishment must be broken, and I regret less than ever having done it. First simply by professional reflex, since I found myself dealing with a question on which you have written a great deal and for a long time. Your 1963 book, *Three Faces of Fascism*, interested me very much when it appeared in French, now thirty years ago! Beyond this respect for the rules of our profession, your books raise too many problems essential to the understanding of the twentieth century for their summary condemnation not to hide a great deal of blindness.

The Obsession with Nazism

In effect, this blindness has its most obvious roots in *the obsession with Nazism*, which has dominated the democratic tradition for more than a half-century, as if the Second World War were an inexhaustible illustration of its historical and moral significance.

In fact, rather than diminish as the events at its source become more distant in time, this obsession has grown in the intervening fifty years, as the essential criteria for distinguishing the "good" citizens from the "bad" (to borrow the vocabulary of the French Revolution for an instant), to the point that it has even provoked the rebirth of imaginary fascisms, which are necessary in order to find later incarnations of the defeat of Hitler and Mussolini.

The crimes of Nazism were so great and became so universally apparent (at the end of the war), that the pedagogical perpetuation of their memory plays an obviously useful and even necessary role long after the generations that committed them have disappeared. Public opinion sensed more or less correctly that these crimes had something specifically modern about them, that they were linked to certain traits of our societies, and that a repetition of them needed to be all the more carefully avoided. This feeling of fear in relation to ourselves formed the basis of the antifascist obsession and, at the same time, the best of its justifications.

But this fear was also used by the communist movement from the start. And this utilization was never so apparent and powerful as in the aftermath of the Second World War, when, through the defeat of Hitler, History seemed to give a certificate of democracy to Stalin, as if antifascism, a purely negative definition, sufficed for freedom. By this, the antifascist obsession added a disastrous effect to its necessary role; it made the analysis of communist regimes difficult, if not impossible.

You believe that this blindness is particularly complete on the German Left, and even in Germany in general, for obvious reasons in some cases. Nazism was a German apocalypse that wrenched your country from its tradition and exposed it to an unprecedented misfortune, compounded by a general condemnation. It is easy to understand how collective political sentiments were mobilized almost exclusively by this national tragedy. It is also easy to see why the anticommunist argument became taboo, since it had already been useful to Hitler. The same thing can be seen, *mutatis mutandis*, in Italy, for the same reasons.

So Interdependent Are They . . .

However, I am not sure that you don't push the analysis of German uniqueness a little too far in this respect in your letter. After all, in my country as well, and in democratic Europe, fascism, *a fortiori* in its Nazi form, was a more or less taboo subject for the historian. I mean that the moral condemnation directed against the two regimes precluded not only studying them, but also understanding the popularity they enjoyed between the two wars. And the taboo that impeded all types of comparative analysis, and even the idea of an interdependence between communism and fascism, was just as great, even if it did not have the same historical or cultural reasons.

In France as well, ideas of this type were disqualified as pure Cold War instruments, whereas they appear so often in authors of the 1930s. It seems to me that from this perspective, the difference between your country and mine is more one of degree than of substance. In France the existence of a venerable democratic revolutionary tradition fed the communist illusion more than it pierced its secrets. And the victory of the "antifascist" coalition of the "Popular Front" in 1936 contributed to this as well.[1] In fact, the existence of an "antifascist" Marxist tradition is not foreign to German culture; it is this tradition that the former GDR [German Democratic Republic] used for intellectual legitimization.

Whatever the respective situation of French and German historians faced with understanding the twentieth century, it is clear that the obsession with fascism, therefore with antifascism, was used by the communist movement as the means to hide its true nature from the eyes of public opinion. The critique of this vision, which took on the force of a theology, must be carried out so as to enter into the real history of fascism and communism. In this, you have shown the way, and this will be clear to everyone with the passage of time, in ten or fifty years.

I, like you, am seeking to understand the strange fascination that these two great ideological and political movements, fascism and communism, held in our century, although I come at it from a different angle. You put the spotlight on fascism, whereas I have tried to understand the seduction of the communist idea in the minds of people. But no one can understand one of the two camps without considering the other, so interdependent are they in representations, passions, and global historical reality.

The Hatred of the Bourgeoisie

This interdependence can be studied in many ways—from the perspective of ideas, from the vantage point of passions or of regimes, for example. The first aspect leads to studying how democratic politics were torn between the idea of the universal and that of the particular, or, to use your terms, between transcendence and immanence, a philosophical antagonism that fed passions of reciprocal hostility. The fascist movement fed on anticommunism, the communist movement on antifascism. But both shared a hatred for the bourgeois world, which allowed them to unite. Finally, the comparison between the two regimes, Stalinian Bolshevik and Hitlerian, has inspired a vast literature since the 1930s, about which Hannah Arendt made her best-known argument (but not the only one).[2]

In my book I tried to do justice to all these aspects. As you well understood, in this regard I am closer to your interpretation than to Arendt's. The idea of totalitarianism, if it permits the comparison of what is comparable in the regimes of Stalin and Hitler, is incapable of explaining their very different origins. The interpretation that consists of following the "historico-genetic" development of fascist and communist regimes, to use your terms, seems more convincing to me and of greater interpretive force. However, I diverge from you on an important point. I think you insist too much on the "reactive" character of fascism to communism, that is, on the posterior character of its appearance in chronological order and on its being shaped by the precedent of October. I myself see two potential figures of modern democracy in both movements, which arise from the same history.

Only a Part of the Truth

Lenin takes power in 1917, Mussolini in 1922, Hitler fails in 1923 to succeed ten years later. Thus, ten years later, Mussolinian fascism can be considered a "reaction" to an Italian-style Bolshevism, also arising out of the war and more or less modeled on the Russian example. In the same manner, Nazism can be made into a response to the German obsession with the Komintern, a response along the dictatorial and revolutionary lines of communism. This type of interpretation has some validity in the sense that the fear of communism fed fascist parties, but to me only partially, because it has the disadvantage of masking what was endogenous and particular to the fascist regimes while overemphasizing what they both fought against. The cultural elements from which they fashioned a "doctrine" for themselves existed before the First World War and therefore the October Revolution. Mussolini did not wait until 1917 to invent the union of the revolutionary and national idea. The German extreme Right, and even the entire Right, did not need communism to hate democracy. The national Bolsheviks admired Stalin. I concede that Hitler privileged the hatred of Bolshevism, but as a final product of the democratic bourgeois world. In fact, certain of his close accomplices, such as Goebbels, made no mystery of hating Paris and London more than Moscow.

Therefore, I think that the thesis of fascism as a "reactive" movement against communism only explains part of the phenomenon; it fails to explain the differences between Italian and German fascism. Above all, it does not allow us to understand origins and traits that the two fascisms share with the detested regime. I have explained myself at length on this subject in chapter 6 of my book (notably pp. 197–98), in order to spare you what risks being a mere repetition. I will add, however, that in assigning both a chronological and a causal meaning to the precedence of Bolshevism to fascism, you expose yourself to the accusation of wanting to exonerate Nazism in a certain sense. The claim that "the gulag preceded Auschwitz" is neither false nor insignificant, but it is not a cause-effect link.

I also diverge from you in your analysis of the "rational motivations" of Hitlerian anti-Semitism. Not that the existence of a great number of Jews in the different administrative staffs of world communism isn't a known fact (with the Russian party at the top of the list). But Hitler and the Nazis didn't need this to give substance to their hatred of the Jews, which was older than the October Revolution. In fact, before them, Mussolini, whom they so admired, had led anticommunist fascism to victory without anti-Semitism. Here I find the disagreement that separates us regarding the origins of Nazism, which are older and more specifically German than a simple hostility to Bolshevism will allow. Before having been the scapegoats of Bolshevism, the Jews were the scapegoats of democracy. And even if it is true that they expose themselves to this curse through their privileged relation with modern universalism, they do it in two roles, as bourgeois and as communists, the first image preceding the second (in fact you yourself emphasize that if they are numerous in the communist ranks, they are also on the front lines of the century's liberal anticommunism). Here again I come upon German culture's particular violence against modern democracy, which I consider a contribut-

ing factor in the rise of Nazism and which exists prior
to Bolshevism. What you call the "rational core" of Nazi
anti-Semitism is rather, in my eyes, the imaginary super-
imposition of two successive but not incompatible incarnations of modernity by the Jews. It seems to me that the
reading of *Mein Kampf* confirms this interpretation. In it,
Bolshevism is only the last avatar of the Jewish project of
world domination.

But the question is too vast and too central not to return
to it in our future exchanges.

Respectfully yours,
FRANÇOIS FURET

                                        Paris, April 3, 1996

4

From the Gulag to Auschwitz

Ernst Nolte

MY DEAR COLLEAGUE,

Allow me first to express, in all objectivity, my admiration for the courage you demonstrate. If even university scholars of the Anglo-Saxon world reacted to you as you suggest at the beginning of your letter, how much greater must be the indignation and anger in France and Italy.

Moreover, no one forced you to adopt a favorable position toward my work in the long note on pages 195–96 of your book. If it is true that it would have triggered strong opposition in any case, no doubt the most negative emotional reactions would not have found anything to feed on if you hadn't mentioned the author "demonized" by the Left in Europe. You must have obeyed only scientific honesty, which refuses to hide what, in one way or another, played an important role in the elaboration of your own ideas. There is something extraordinarily consoling about the fact that a motive of this kind can show itself in spite of all the suspicions and among so many motivations that have nothing to do with scientific work.

I am still sometimes surprised by the contemporary Left's show of aggressivity, and I can't even think about it without finding something ridiculous in it. Is it really so difficult to note that an internal necessity pushes us toward the historico-genetic conception of the theory of totalitarianism if we subscribe to the basic points of the Marxist interpretation of the twentieth century without accepting the claim of Marxism, and thus of communism, of having the market on absolute truth? What have all the Marxist theories underlined most strongly if not that fascisms were desperate reactions of the bourgeoisie, condemned to failure in the face of the victorious rise of the socialist and proletarian movement? But if this idea is not founded on knowledge of the inexorable laws of universal history, if it is, on the contrary, only a weapon used by a political party in its battles, a weapon that *doesn't* fundamentally distinguish it from other parties—even though its particular status must be acknowledged—if it is based on an insufficient understanding of "bourgeois society," and if its final failure is nothing more than coincidence, the picture of the period is totally different, even if certain essential lines of interpretation are preserved. The historico-genetic version of the theory of totalitarianism is much closer to the Marxist analysis than is the "classic" or structural version, and obviously it is this proximity which arouses so much anger.

Understandable Reactions

From another perspective, I do not want to deny that the hostile reactions are nevertheless understandable. To be close to the Marxist conception at once implies a certain proximity to the fascist interpretation, which is, in so obvious a manner, profoundly dependent on the Marxist analysis. If the communist movement is judged illegitimate, if one goes so far as to see in it an effort to "assassinate Western civilization," the scales of historical justice will unequivocally tip in favor of fascisms. In any case, this *is not* what I think, and when, in your argument published in *Le Débat*, you seem to insinuate that I would reproach you for your former involvement in the PCF [French Communist Party], I can only disagree.[1] If the workers' movement in the nineteenth century had not existed to rise up against the precocious and terrible forms of the market and competitive economy, if the First World War had provoked only reflections of a pragmatic order without the appearance of militant pacifism, one would have to despair of humanity. Even if its utopian illusions were shattered by History, the Marxist-communist movement did have greatness, and those who remained complete strangers to it must today blame themselves rather than those who got involved. Because of this, as early as *Three Faces of Fascism* I explicitly proved the fascist Mussolini right against his one-time companions to the extent that he predicted a great longevity for capitalism; but I have never had the least doubt that I saw in Marxism a more original movement, the product of very old roots, and in fascisms, a reaction of a secondary order, artificial in large part, based on postulates. This is why all of those who impute "anticommunism" to me and consider it the primary motive of my work are wrong. At the most, one could speak of antiabsolutism, that is, a refusal of all claim to an absolute truth. But the claim to an absolute truth such as Hitler asserted, the idea that the Jews "pulled the strings of world history," doesn't even warrant denial. In my eyes, it simply deserves to be rejected.

Of course, it is safer to refrain from all forms of proximity to National Socialism and to put a negative slant on all that National Socialism saw as positive, and vice versa—for example, as is the case of the prevalent thesis in my country of a "German uniqueness," which reached its paroxysm in Nazism. Recently I was able to observe again, and precisely in the context of our discussion, to what point an apparently negligible imprecision can easily give rise to justified criticisms.

In my contribution to *Le Débat* I wrote: "because we insist on considering the Jews the victims of an infamous undertaking, and not as actors in a tragedy" (p. 146). In this form the statement is erroneous. It even provokes indignation. But the original German text said something different: "because we do not want to consider the Jews as actors participating in a tragedy, but solely [!] as victims of a wicked undertaking."[2] The idea of "participation" *[Mit* in *Mitwirkende]* as well as the restrictive nuance of the adverb "solely" *[nur]* gave the sentence a much less absolute character, and what was in all probability a simple oversight in translation brought about a serious modification of my meaning.

I needn't tell you that I take criticism from you far more seriously than from anyone else. You think that I insist too much on the reactive character of fascisms, and that in doing this I neglect their roots—the anti-Semitism of Hitler, for example, would have been virulent long before the First World War and therefore cannot be a reaction to Bolshevism.

A Causal Nexus

You are absolutely right to think that National Socialism could not be deduced exclusively from a reaction to the Bolshevik movement, that on the contrary there existed, even before the war, a brutal German nationalism, and that explicit intentions of extermination of the Jews were even expressed in the program of one party. A glance into your area of specialization, the French Revolution and its prehistory, will perhaps help clarify the remark. Well before 1789, tendencies opposed to the Enlightenment existed in Germany too, and the criticisms leveled at their partisans were very similar to those later aimed at the Jacobins. Nevertheless, these tendencies took on another character when the king was condemned to death and executed; things became "really serious." From my perspective, in almost the same manner, things became "really serious" for Hitler when he was confronted with the reality of what he called the "bloody Russian dictatorship" and "the destruction of the national intelligentsia." I believe that only in this way is it possible to establish a "causal nexus" between the gulag and Auschwitz. Of course, "causal nexus" doesn't imply the same restricting causal articulation present in the natural sciences, and which occurs beyond human conceptions and opinions. If the views of Hitler and all his close accomplices are put to one side, then there is no "causal nexus" between the gulag and Auschwitz, and as far as one can judge, there would have been no Auschwitz. However, it is permissible to speak of a more subtle nexus: if someone, no matter who, promised to oppose Bolshevism with a regime "as determined and consistent," something had to exist that was analogous to the very considerable "abolition of classes," something as clearly called for by ideology and for which the principal object could hardly be any group but the Jews.

The assertion that in History the Jews had always been at the source of "all inequality and all social injustice" was obviously irrational, even ridiculous, no more than a bizarre counterpart of the thesis of the first socialists and Marxists that denounced the destructive character of private property. But the "rational core" of Nazi anti-Judaism consists in the factual reality of the large role played by a certain number of personalities of Jewish origin at the center of the communist and socialist movement, evidently because of universalist and Messianic traditions proper to historical Judaism. "Rational core" does not necessarily mean "legitimate core": "rational" means something that can be apprehended in an intelligible manner or that can be represented in an immanent manner. In the Middle Ages, anti-Semitism existed in the fabrications regarding the use of Christian blood or "ritual murders," but we can consider the pogroms of the Jewish monopoly on financial lending (which arose more from necessity than from desire) as a rational core. It is possible to rationally understand these rebellions against the "usurer," but they were no doubt unjustified because they threatened the development of the market economy. To me, Nazi anti-Semitism also had a rational core in this sense, but it wasn't legitimate either, because it threatened a possible and positive development—the passage from a workers' movement to social democracy, in which certain Jews such as Otto Bauer or Léon Blum played a central role. For this reason, the idea of considering Nazism as initially

a reaction against Bolshevism and thus vindicating it
seems unjustified. Nazism was certainly not just a reaction against Bolshevism, but an excessive one, and as a
general rule, excess in what is justified at the outset leads
to the unjustifiable. As German nationalism, Nazism was
no less legitimate than French or Italian nationalism,
but when it took the form of a denial of rights, as was
stipulated in point 4 of the program of its party, it became
illegitimate excess.

Legitimate Objections

But again I insist that I don't reject certain objections
outright, even when they are less carefully justified than
yours are. In particular, I can't contest the legitimacy of
asking ourselves if, so short a time after Auschwitz, we
shouldn't put off all questions concerning the "participation" of the Jews since this type of questioning would
certainly reopen wounds and, if need be, could even be
used by current anti-Semites. This could be the reason for
advancing exclusively the "victim" character of the Jews.
In doing so, haven't we closed the perspective on what was
really important? The historical greatness of the Jews—
"people of God" or "people of humanity"—doesn't authorize
putting the Jews on the same level as the gypsies,[3] who,
in fact, were only victims. Are we not as unjust toward
the Jews as the Germans were *(per impossibile)* when
we assert that all anti-Germanism and all anti-Judaism,
the beginnings of which appear in antiquity, are founded
on simple prejudices? Wouldn't asking oneself about the
"rational core" of Nazi anti-Judaism open a way to the

adequate understanding of other "anti" attitudes that we can deplore from a moral standpoint, but which nevertheless constitute such an essential part of universal history?

I wouldn't be very surprised if many critics went so far as to assert that here I pleaded the cause "for anti-Semitism." Actually, I am only arguing that we take certain oppositions seriously, for example, the opposition between universalism and particularism, which, of course, was not absolute in nature but "dialectical," and which, I am convinced, is still so today. If I am not mistaken, in your book you yourself define as an "illusion" precisely the fact that universalism can deny all legitimacy to particularism and in this way annihilate it. What dangers for the world, and above all for the discipline of history, lie in the unique absolute exigency expressed today, that of universalist egalitarianism? This is something that still requires much thought.

I await your response with pleasure and send you my deepest regards.

Your colleague,
ERNST NOLTE

Berlin, May 9, 1996

5

The Dialectical Relationship of Fascism and Communism

François Furet

My Dear Colleague,

It seems to me your second letter clarifies and reduces the area of our disagreement without abolishing it.

Let me tell you first, in regard to you personally, how I came to write this long note on you. When I started working on *Le Passé d'une illusion* in 1989, I had read your books as they were published because of my interest in the mid-1960s in the three volumes of *Three Faces of Fascism*. I didn't immediately feel the need to reread them, because I was working on the communist idea and not on the fascist idea or movement. But after a year or two, as my work advanced, I constantly encountered the problem of the dialectical relationship of communism and fascism, the mutual engendering and reinforcing of the two great mass ideologies arising from the First World War. This is what led me once again to take up your work, which I could have simply cited like all the others that figure in the notes of my book. But your work has a double particularity because it attempts to present a general interpretation of twentieth-century European history, and because it was not ignored but attacked by silence and excommunication. Because of this, it warrants separate commentary. As a historian, I have always found myself revisiting the historiography of the question I wish to research. Given the current state of available works on the periods of the two world wars in Europe, your writings seem to me to be at the top of the list of those that should be discussed by anyone undertaking work on the events of this period and the problems they raise.

Why? Because the only serious way to approach the study of the two original ideologies and political movements that appeared at the beginning of our century, Marxist-Leninist communism and fascism in its Italian and German forms, is to take them *together* as the two faces of an acute crisis of liberal democracy that arose with the First World War. This critique of the modern democratic idea in the name of a former "organic" society on the Right and in the name of a "future" socialist society on the Left is a longstanding reality of European political culture. What is new with the First World War is the extreme radicalization of this double critique in Leninism and fascism. Leninism draws its strength from realizing the old hope of the workers' movement, even at the price of a formidable improbability. Fascism's strength lies in recovering for the enemies of democratic ideas the fascination of a *tomorrow*, of a future society, no longer a past one. Since *homo democraticus* appeared on the European scene, liberal civilization has denied him a real human community, most powerfully embodied in a universal association of producers or a national body of citizens. The two forms appear in real history at the end of the First World War.

Up to this point I believe that we are in agreement, and I concur that this "genealogical" approach to the European tragedy is more interesting than the "structural" comparison of Hitlerian and Stalinian totalitarianisms. The point communism and fascism have in common is the fundamental political deficit of modern democracy. The different types of totalitarian regimes that are established in their name share the will to put an end to this deficit by restoring the main role to political decisions and by integrating the masses into one party through the constant assertion of their ideological orthodoxy. The fact that the two ideologies proclaim themselves to be in a situation of radical conflict does not prevent them from reinforcing each other by this very hostility—the communist nourishes his faith with antifascism, and the fascist his with anticommunism. And both fight the same enemy, bourgeois democracy. The communist sees it as the breeding ground of fascism, while the fascist sees it as the antechamber of Bolshevism, but they both fight to destroy it.

At this point of analysis, you introduce a distinction based on chronology, but you give this distinction a causal meaning—that is, that the Bolshevik revolution precedes fascism, which defines itself, by contrast, as an anti-Marxist reaction. And you are completely correct to write in your letter that in doing so, you take up, at least partially, the Marxist interpretation of the twentieth century, which, in effect, considered fascist movements a response of bourgeois democracies to the Bolshevik threat in the era of imperialism in the final stage of market production.

If we leave aside this obviously erroneous diagnosis of the imminent collapse of capitalism, it remains that the definition of fascism as a reactive movement against the Bolshevik revolution is fundamental in Marxist-Leninist analysis, as it is in yours—a proximity that perhaps explains in part the hostile passions your thesis has provoked in the European Left.

But while I agree that Bolshevism and fascism are interdependent, I don't believe that they can be interpreted solely on the basis of their successive appearance in History. The communists did so in order to underline the unique and radically new character of the October Revolution as opposed to the derivative nature of fascism, the last avatar of capitalist domination, basically identical to all regimes that are products of this domination. You, on the other hand, were suspected by your adversaries of seeking to exonerate fascism, and particularly Nazism, by reducing it to a fear of Bolshevism. In your second letter, you reject this accusation with two arguments, which, if I am not mistaken, I have not found in your recent writings, but which come, most likely, from your earlier works on Marxism. The first consists of the assertion of the "greatness" of the Marxist-Leninist illusion, because of its universalism—a greatness that relegates the fascist idea to a secondary importance, "secondary and in part artificial." The second is that you acknowledge the existence of cultural roots of fascism prior to the war and independent of Bolshevism. It is true that you minimize their role by comparing them to counterrevolutionary ideas in France in their incubation period, before the execution of Louis XVI.

The Role of the War

I am not sure that in the French Revolution the death of Louis XVI is the watershed that you suggest; I would tend to see a more important factor in the religious schism beginning in 1791. But this question is secondary to our discussion. The essential thing is that by acknowledging the existence of a fascist or fascistic doctrinal body already constituted before 1914, you considerably weaken the thesis of a purely reactive, anti-Bolshevik fascism. If you try to save this thesis by distinguishing between the latent power of an idea and the historical force that it becomes following a play of given circumstances—an indispensable distinction for all historians—then I will tell you that the war of 1914 alone, probably plays a bigger role in the "actualization" of fascism than does even the October Revolution. How else could the impact of defeat in Germany or of national humiliation in Italy be explained? I insist on the idea of the political autonomy of fascism in relation to Bolshevism, or if you prefer, on its endogenous character within European culture, because, as I explain in the first and the sixth chapters of my book, fascism is the solution finally available to the impasses of counter-revolutionary ideas (pp. 208–11). It enables the recovery of the attraction of revolution in the service of a radical critique of the principles of 1789.

Its galvanizing effect on the masses comes from making the national idea absolute—as, in an opposite sense, the mythology of October 17 found support by rendering the universalist idea absolute. Even in Nazi Germany, nationalist passion was what tied the German people most strongly to the Hitlerian adventure to the very end. However, in this case, Hitler made this passion absolute in the extreme form of a biologico-historical election of a superior race, called to dominate the world. It was in the name of this "theory," superimposed on an exacerbated nationalism (which sufficed to feed Italian fascism), that the German army carried out the massacre of European Jews during the Second World War.

The Massacre of European Jews

On behalf of Hitler and the Nazis, you wish to attribute what you call a "rational core" to this massacre. But from the examples you present, I am unable to understand what you mean by "rational." If you mean by this "intelligible to reason," let me remind you that even the most insane beliefs are intelligible to reason, and that the imputation of all social injustices to the Jews is no more "irrational" than the assimilation of Bolshevism to a plot in which they pull the stings. In both cases one starts from a true fact—the existence of big capitalists who are Jewish or the presence of a certain number of Jews in the early Bolshevik leadership—in order to draw absurd conclusions that can lead to crimes. In the case of Hitler and his accomplices, however, the Jews not only incarnate Bolshevism in their eyes but also stateless capitalism. This allows the Nazis to magically unite in the same hatred a single people who presumably incarnate two contradictory ideas and social regimes. The historian can discern here again where this powerful and perverse mirage is born. For many reasons, of which I do

not have the time here to make even a summary inventory, the Jews are the people of the modern world most
attracted to universalism—thus at once to liberalism and
to communism—after having been the most persecuted
and ghettoized people of Christian Europe, yet enclosed in
the promise of their divine election, which allowed them
to survive. But this most extraordinary trait of modern
(or "assimilated," according to the French term) European
Judaism before the Second World War doesn't warrant
the attribution of any "rational core" to the belief that in
eliminating the Jews, communism and capitalism would
be eliminated once and for all. This belief remains completely "irrational" (from the point of view of its examination by reason), even if the historian can find its sources
in the experience of the past, transfigured by ideological passion.

The Specificity of Passions and Crimes

Because you write me that you are sensitive to the general emotion that at this century's end always surrounds
the massacre of Jews by Nazi Germany, allow me to add
that in this area more than in any other, the vocabulary employed must avoid ambiguity. I do not suspect
you either of being anti-Semitic or of wishing to mask
the crime of the Jewish genocide, something to which
your books clearly attest. But why then do you seem to
look for elements of an explanation for it drawn from
another regime, in another country? This is a return to
your thesis that fascism is completely explained as a response to Bolshevism, but it is no more convincing from

this angle than in its general aspect. Anti-Semitism is a
passion that is foreign to the Russian Revolution (even
if, in a later stage, under Stalin, the revolution managed to use it), and I do not believe that one can find
in Hitler's statements the parallel you outline between
the extermination of the Kulaks and that of the Jews.
The parallel history of Bolshevism and fascism, which I
believe, as you do, is necessary to the understanding of
twentieth-century Europe, should not obscure the speci-
ficity of their passions and crimes, which are what identi-
fies each one. If not, how could the intentions of the actors
be explained? Hitler did not need the Soviet precedent
of the liquidation of the Kulaks in order to contemplate,
plan, and recommend the liquidation of the Jews. The way
between the avowed intention and its execution was paved
by war and conquest, without necessary recourse to the
hypothesis of an "imitation" of the anti-Kulak terror of
the early 1930s.

The particular trait of Nazism, as an idea and as a
regime, is its attempt to transform the hatred of the Jews,
a widespread political passion throughout Europe at the
time, into a general massacre of the Jews, a physical
liquidation of a people considered as not belonging to the
human race. This doesn't mean that the extraordinary
history of Judaism can be reduced to the tragedy of a
scapegoat people, a victim of modernity; nor that national
sentiments are without honor, or that the role of nations
in the development of a culture is exhausted. I agree with
you on this. But this conviction obliges the historian to
look at the "absolutizing" of national emotions, to use your
expression, as a specific curse of German history, which in

my eyes remains the most enigmatic phenomenon of the twentieth century.

I am glad that this correspondence affords me the opportunity to discuss these difficult questions with you.

Best regards,
FRANÇOIS FURET

June 24, 1996

6

On Revisionism

Ernst Nolte

MY DEAR COLLEAGUE,

I don't think that in the matter of the "rational core" of
Nazi anti-Semitism we should be satisfied with an "agreement to disagree."[1] This is why I would like to explain
my concept by an example and at the same time show
that several paths exist that lead from the "rational" to
the "irrational."

The Rational Core

The "rational core" can be expressed in a simple propo-
sition that would state approximately the following: men
and women of Jewish origin took part in the intellectual
development and organizations of ideology and socialist
movements in Europe in a much higher than average
proportion and also in the conquest of power and early
period of Bolshevik domination in Russia. This propo-
sition doesn't refer to what would only be a theoretical

investigation but to a reality. This is undeniable, certainly between you and me, because, in one form or another, this assertion is found in many works of specialists who, as a general rule, give a clear explanation of this fact.

Fundamentally this assertion is the counterpart of another, just as irrefutable. Among Nobel laureates, scholars of Jewish origin are represented in much higher than average proportion. This fact is ordinarily and rightfully understood as a mark of distinction. But it is not inconceivable that this praise can be transformed into a criticism, even an accusation, if the antiscientific tendency, a strain existing in "public opinion" everywhere in the Western world, were to gain force and become radicalized. However, it would be almost impossible for just any fanatic to hit upon the idea of asserting that the natural sciences, even science in general, could be a Jewish *product*. According to our current criteria, it would be simply absurd, irrational to be exact, even though the initial observation was objectively correct and therefore completely rational. In addition, at the same time this would be to overvalue in an inconceivable manner a single and even small group of men. A world phenomenon such as science cannot be attributed to the activity of a single group, no matter how gifted, who would be the "cause."

This passing from the rational to the irrational in regard to science, which even today seems impossible, actually did occur in the context of socialism and the Bolsheviks. Of course, it only appeared in the enemies of socialism, but they represented a considerable number of diverse men. In principle, today it would be just as possible to evaluate positively the overrepresentation of the Jews in the elaboration of a phenomenon of incontestable global importance. This is what began to happen early on, but established socialism did not accept these attempts because, with reason, it could not see more than a partial cause of its successes in this collaboration with the Jews. However, the adversaries converted the tendentially positive evaluation into its opposite, and by the end of the nineteenth century, they wanted to see the "Jewish revolutionaries," such as Marx and Lassalle, as the principal founders of socialism. But it was only after the Bolsheviks' conquest of power that the idea that the Jews were responsible for the disastrous upheaval could emerge. Thus, in very real terms this conversion of a rational interrogation to an irrational assertion occurred, whereas in the case of science it can only occur within the context of a reflexive hypothesis.

But the irrational interpretation was still far from the totally irrational crime, which, in exterminating precisely the poorest and most defenseless of the Jewish people, was supposed to settle not only the "Jewish question" but also sweep away socialism—more exactly, internationalist socialism, Marxist socialism—and, finally, "modernity." A series of proofs exists that confirmed anti-Semites were indignant about the extermination of the Jews in the East and tried to oppose it within their means. This crime could only be set in motion at the moment when a fanatical anti-Semite, for reasons that had little to do with anti-Semitism, became absolute master of a large state and thus of a powerful attendant machinery. Without the intention of this central figure, who was Hitler, there could not have been a Final Solution, and this is why even today I ascribe to "intentionalism," which is practically disqualified in our discipline. But to me the horrifying and irrational result began from a pertinent observation, and the passage from the rational to irrational can be reconstructed in a rational manner from it.

If I understand you correctly, true irrationality still consists for you in the fact that the Jews were simultaneously made responsible for two social systems that were diametrically opposed in reality, the Bolshevik planned economy and the capitalist market economy. But may I remind you that already in the nineteenth century, completely serious and reasonable people, even if they were certainly "conservative," supported the idea that socialism and capitalism were just two sides of the same coin, both equally opposed to the Christian state of the European tradition. And in our day don't the Islamic fundamentalists, as well as the pioneers of an "Asian path," make the same argument in essence? Also, in a positive vein this time, isn't the distinction made by numerous leftist intellectuals in the West between Bolshevism, which is based in spite of everything on a "humanist idea," and fascism, which incarnated an ideology hostile to humanity, based on the same idea? Here again, it is not the observation at the outset that is irrational, but only the illegitimate results the Nazis drew from it in this particular form, that is, that there must be an identifiable, ethnically defined people responsible for the fact in question.

In my opinion, the irrational interpretation is not of "German" origin. Nor did it only emerge in 1917. I don't agree at all with the opinion that fascism was "exclusively a reaction against Bolshevism." Almost half of my book *Three Faces of Fascism* is devoted to the prehistory of fascism and Nazism and deals with the period before 1914. However, its focus is not the "German" tradition but the "counterrevolutionary" one common to all Europe. This is why, to me, Gobineau is more important than Theodor Fritsch and even Heinrich von Treitschke, and the dedication of Gobineau's work to the king of Hanover makes it clear that had he been living in 1917, he would have considered the "subversive movements" he speaks of to be a prefiguration of Bolshevism.[2]

I know that for a long time there has been criticism of making fascism *"in its time"* a research theme and considering it a European phenomenon because doing so would objectively "excuse Germany." But I thought, and I continue to think with the same conviction, that we go astray when we want to confine an essential current of the period to a single state and a unique national tradition, a period that, according to everyone, is not characterized by "globalization" only from 1945 on. To take this path would not be so different from the interpretation that wishes to make the "Jewish people" the founders of socialism and Bolshevism. I'm not erasing the differences that surely exist between nations any more than I equate "radical fascism," which took power only in Germany, with the "normal fascism" of Italy. Nor should one dissolve the link between the irrational crime and the rational observation on which it is based in order to make this crime the totally incomprehensible result of an "absolute evil."

Two Critical Remarks

Allow me two critical remarks on several of the sentences in your letter.

You say that you do not suspect me of being anti-Semitic nor of wanting to "excuse the crime of genocide of the

Jews," but apparently you don't consider this suspicion
completely absurd since I went in search of the cause of
genocide in another country and not in the homeland of
the criminals, that is, in Germany. But doesn't it follow
that a historian whose research focus is anti-Semitism is
no more anti-Semitic than a historian who focuses on the
American, English, or French Revolutions is revolutionary? One, like the other, is under the same obligation—
to approach his subject with detachment, motivated by a
desire for objectivity, in no instance content to express hostile remarks, however clear his own conclusions might be.
Unfortunately, in our day the notion of "anti-Semitism" is
one of the most distorted and misused of terms. It is a completely different thing to direct accusations against "the
Jews" and to criticize this or that (mostly self-proclaimed)
protagonist, like Elie Wiesel. If these two approaches both
arise from anti-Semitism, "freedom of thought" is out of
the question. In 1981, when I was invited to Hebrew University in Jerusalem, to my great astonishment I read a
letter in the *Jerusalem Post* from a Jewish woman reader
who complained of the anti-Semitism of her neighbors,
who, unlike her, were Orthodox Jews.

I believe in making distinctions within anti-Semitism
and in taking each of the phenomena designated as such
seriously, that is, to avoid substituting invectives for attempts to understand. Not everyone approves of such a
postulate, but I don't see how historians can contradict it.

You write further on that in the name of making the
national ideal absolute, "the German army carried out
the massacre of European Jews." I'm convinced that you
would raise an objection if a journal of the radical Left
wrote that "the French police" participated with alacrity

in the deportation of French Jews.[3] If the "German army" had been driven by a desire to murder with regard to the Jews, there would have been no need to create the *Einsatzgruppen* of the SS and the police, and the Auschwitz commander would not have been a high-ranking SS officer. It is not as a German but as a historian and as a man that I can't help feeling bitter when in Germany they organize an exhibition on the "crimes of the Wehrmacht," and when they ceaselessly deplore thirty thousand death sentences pronounced by military justice. This is not because I wish to remain silent about the horrible crimes perpetuated within the Wehrmacht, nor because I would find it just to pronounce a death sentence to punish a disparaging opinion with regard to the "Führer," but because what occurred on the Soviet side—the crimes of the GPU, the tens of millions of executions and sentences for "cowardice," even for "sympathy for the enemy"—is completely bracketed and presented as simply nonexistent.

I ask myself sometimes why I am criticized for what is so close to being a platitude in my eyes. Recently while scanning a series of citations from my old readings, I came upon a sentence of Merleau-Ponty from a text published in 1947. Concerning fascism, he says that it is "mimicry of Bolshevism" except in what is truly essential—the theory of the proletariat. This "theory of the proletariat" is obviously exactly what is called the "utopian" part of Bolshevism almost everywhere today. Therefore, today Merleau-Ponty should write that fascism is an imitation of Bolshevism, an imitation lacking this utopian part, and he could certainly add that this utopian element could be qualified as "humanist," in contrast to the antihumanist motives of fascism and, above all, of Nazism. I agree with

Merleau-Ponty on this point, and I am persuaded that you would too—this is why I think that what characterizes the current situation is a violent criticism of what is, in fact, "nothing very particular."

The Question of Revisionism

Actually, there are obviously profound reasons why what appears banal from a certain point of view meets with so much resistance in the case we are concerned with. The long held conviction that Marxist socialism and even Leninist Bolshevism were absolutely different from fascism and totally opposed to it must be mentioned first. Of course, today "Stalinism" has been abandoned everywhere, but the old conviction remains in diverse versions and in diverse watered down forms, from reformed communists to well into the liberal camp. It must be acknowledged that there is also a "rational core" to this conviction, and neither one of us used "identification" in our analysis. But the difference of opinion reaches its emotional extreme when the question concerns the actual magnitude of the "holocaust," or its existence or nonexistence. Here anger and indignation are most understandable, because, in what is called revisionism, it seems motivated only by an impudent denial of tangible facts, testified to in an extensive manner. This indignation can extend to the position I outlined in my work *Streitpunkte* and is summed up in the simple thesis that revisionist arguments must be answered by arguments and not legal action. I am very interested in knowing your position on this question.

But allow me first to explain why the question of revisionism has become so important for me in recent years. In it I see a challenge to the first and most powerful of my beliefs, that is, my basic hypothesis. At the beginning of the 1960s, while I was preparing my book *Three Faces of Fascism*, I did not go to the archives of the state museum of Auschwitz to study documents concerning the construction of the camp, and I did not interview any witnesses. I was aware only of the most important written sources, such as the declarations of Kurt Gerstein and Rudolf Höss, the book of Eugen Kogon, as well as the published acts of the Nuremberg trial. That seemed to suffice since no one at the time questioned the reality of the extermination of millions of people and the use of gas, not even the attorneys of the accused during the big Auschwitz trial getting underway at that time. I didn't yet know the name Rassinier.[4] But I did something that wasn't obvious at the time. I studied the primary sources of Hitler's "conception of the world," his first letters, his first speeches, and the writing of Dietrich Eckart, the long-forgotten poet Hitler saw as a mentor, and the articles of Alfred Rosenberg published in the little magazine *Auf gut deutsch*, the essays of Erwin von Scheubner-Richter, the former diplomat that Hitler judged "irreplaceable" after he was killed in the putsch of 1923.

It was at this time that I made one of several discoveries to my credit: a pamphlet titled *Bolshevism from Moses to Lenin: A Dialogue Between Adolf Hitler and Myself*, which had no author's name but was no doubt written by Dietrich Eckart. Even today I consider this text by far the most important and the most instructive of the "conversations with Hitler," because all the later partners, such as Otto Strasser and Hermann Rauschning, were secondary collaborators, whereas, according to his statements, Hitler considered Eckart his "guiding star." This reading bolstered my earlier conviction, drawn from the reading of *Mein Kampf*, that Hitler was truly a fanatical ideologue for whom anticommunism and anti-Semitism were united to a previously unprecedented degree, something the pamphlet already makes clear. To the extent that Hitler was a sociobiologist for whom peoples and races were the ultimate founding reality, "living substances of flesh and blood," nothing other than "Auschwitz" could be the result, as the supreme postulate of this counterideology, and as far as I know, I was the first who believed it possible to establish that certain early declarations by Hitler, notably a sentence from this "conversation" with Eckart, contained a clear anticipation of the extermination of the Jews.

My entire interpretation turns on this central point. If radical revisionism were right to assert that there was no "holocaust" in the sense of general and systematic measures of extermination decided at the top level of the state (apart from the partisans war carried out with great harshness on both sides in the Soviet Union), and that there were only vast deportations—comparable to the internment of Germans in England and the citizens of Japanese origin in the United States—in which the large number of victims could be blamed on extreme conditions, then I would make the following confession. I considered a politician to be an ideologue animated by a rage to exterminate, a politician who, at times like other politicians, threatened his enemies for psychological reasons, a politician who wanted nothing more with regard to the

"Jewish question" than what the Zionists wished for, that is, the divorce of two peoples after the failure of their effort at a shared life; and by such an interpretation, my own would be invalidated. During the last war it was not two states driven by opposing ideologies, each determined to exterminate the other, but a simple extension of the battles between the great powers of the First World War; Nazism wasn't a "distorted copy of Bolshevism," but led a fight only for the survival of Germany, put on the defensive by world politics. No author voluntarily accepts that his work is ruined, and I therefore have a vital interest in revisionism *not being* right, at least in its radical version. But this is precisely the reason I feel provoked by it. On the other hand, I don't see myself associating with those who want to mobilize the public prosecutors and the police against it. Thus I feel constrained to ask the question of whether revisionism disposes of arguments, or if it is in fact only an uproar tangled in lies.

What is at stake here is neither more nor less than the fundamental quality of the historian. He knows that "revisions" are the daily bread of scientific work and that in the history of the nineteenth and twentieth centuries, "revisionisms" haven't stopped springing up even in the victor's camp, when their ideas enjoyed an apparently unassailable privilege during or following major events. This is what happened after the Civil War and after the First World War. At the outset of the "Cold War" as well, a Western revisionism attacked the West's central thesis that the Soviet Union was responsible for triggering the "East-West" conflict.

The historian also knows that as a general rule certain revisionist theses end up being accepted by the establishment or at least introduced into the discussion. Thus, as far as I know, the previously disparaged assertions of Gar Alperovitz concerning the Cold War currently enjoy wide acceptance. The first atomic bombs targeted Japan less than the Soviet Union.[5] It is impossible to avoid asking oneself if this analogy is equally valid for the "revisionism concerning the Holocaust" of Rassinier, Faurisson, Mattogno, and the *Journal of Historical Review*.

One can't answer solely in the negative except on the condition that until then there was no "research need" or any questionable assertion in the area of the "Final Solution." But this is not the case.

The most important specialists on the Holocaust, all belonging to the "established school," including Raul Hilberg and Yehuda Bauer, participated in a conference in Stuttgart in 1984. On that occasion Bauer criticized the still current and unassailable thesis in Germany that the extermination of the Jews was "decided" at the "Wannsee Conference." Hilberg strongly insisted on the fact that the frequently advanced figure of 2.5 million Jewish victims at Auschwitz was an impossibility, that the number could not surpass 1 million. (Several years later this revision became the official version. On commemorative plaques at Auschwitz, the "four million" was replaced by "from one to one-and-a-half million.") One member of the Berlin Institute of Research on Anti-Semitism indicated that Zyklon B, "which has often been ignored," was frequently used to combat vermin, and that it was indispensable in the camps where typhus was widespread, and he cautioned against "overestimating the number of those who were killed at Auschwitz-Birkenau." Eberhard Jäckel referred to certain indications that Göring and Goebbels and even

Himmler expressed reservations regarding the first mass executions. Hilberg underscored the great importance of "hearsay," declarations that were not based on personal experience but on what others reported, which had played a large role, even among the leadership of the Nazi party machine. No mention was made of the claim that during and immediately following the war, mass executions were carried out by injecting burning vapor into closed rooms while passing electric current on huge plaques or by using quick lime. This silence in the face of assertions of this order amounted to declaring them obviously erroneous, as was also the case, for example, regarding the rumor that soap had been milled from Jewish cadavers, a claim nevertheless repeated recently in Germany in the press releases of a well-known director. Even *de visu* accounts of the 1950s of the high-ranking SS Kurt Gerstein, a member of the Catholic Church, are no longer mentioned in the bibliography of completely orthodox researchers. And we know that Jean-Claude Pressac, recognized as a serious scholar in spite of unusual precedents, recently reduced the number of gas chamber victims at Auschwitz to around half a million.

Similar corrections of detail are not unlike certain assertions that, to my knowledge, were only made by "revisionists." For example, that the first confessions of the Auschwitz commander Höss were extorted under torture, that the high flames coming from the chimneys of the crematoriums observed by numerous eyewitnesses were only optical illusions, that the technical conditions were not in place to carry out the daily cremation of twenty-four thousand cadavers, that the morgues in the camp crematoriums that counted about three hundred "natural"

deaths each day during typhus epidemics were there for
that purpose only and, at least during those periods, could
not be used for mass executions.

Even such theses hardly surprise the historian, made
aware by his daily work that since the time of Herodotus,
large numbers, unless they come from statistical specialists, can only be questionable, and he knows as well that
large crowds assembled in extreme situations and confronted with inexplicable events were, and remain, real
rumor mills. Nevertheless, all these corrections and re-
strictions don't place the core of the matter in doubt, and
the postulate that they should not be excluded from free
scientific examination is appropriate. You know the literature perhaps better than I, and you can show me the
passages where these problems and these doubts were
explained. If I am not mistaken, this has not occurred
in Germany.

The Essential is Incontestable

Two other claims are of a different order. They completely
and fundamentally deny the existence of gas-chamber extermination. The first could lead to a spectacular defeat
of the revisionists if it weren't kept from the public. It
concerns the claim that the morgues of the crematoriums could not have been used as gas chambers because
no significant trace of cyanide could be found in them,
as opposed to the rooms used for the destruction of vermin. The other claim, advanced for some time, maintains
that the openings in the roofs of the crematoriums, which
were necessary to dispense the poison, were made af-

ter the fact, and that even today they were not adapted for pipes.

However, even if these two claims were definitively refuted, it would not suffice to dispense with the question of whether a revisionism that distances itself from provocative agitation and that proceeds by argumentation is not, in fact, an extreme example of revisions that are legitimate in principle and should be accepted as phenomena internal to scientific development. If this were the case, obviously strong criticism of the revisionism in question would be pursued, not excluded. I'm inclined to answer this question in the affirmative because what would science be if it were not always constantly required to carry out its critique of grave scientific errors through extensive work and to discover other cores of truth in the errors themselves!

But to me the statement of Hitler's political testament remains incomparably more probing than all the arguments of revisionism. The guilty one, that is, Judaism, has meanwhile suffered its punishment "even though inflicted by the most humane methods." And I would suggest sending all the revisionists a copy of the commemorative book published by the archives of the Federal Republic on "the victims of the persecution of the Jews under the National Socialist dictatorship in Germany from 1933 to 1945," a two-volume work in which more than one hundred thousand names of men, women, and children are listed with the indication of the place from which the last information on them came. One of the columns shows the fate of each one. These indications don't specify if one was "gassed" or if another "died of typhus" because it is impossible to establish exactly what happened in each case, but they simply state "disappeared" or "died." And most often, but not always, the last place indicated is "Auschwitz." On the whole, this 1,700-page large-format publication is more important and more moving regarding "the essential" and the incontestable than the representations of certain personal fates and the works (however vast) of historians, no matter how sensitive they may be.

If I could make a wish, it would be that one of the well-known experts and archive analysts of the "established school" write a book in which he records without anger or obvious indignation the arguments of the revisionists and analyzes them in detail so that we would finally arrive at a result comparable to earlier examinations of revisionist arguments, and in this form: "It must be acknowledged that . . . but in no way does this call the essence of the matter into doubt."

But I consider the claim fundamentally false that if the essential is irrefutable, no particular claim need be further examined, and that all the doubts can only come from bad intentions. I think that the core of the matter is threatened when the shell of the discussion is removed, certainly not the factual character of the core, but the rank and importance accorded it.

If the matter had to follow another course, if we insist on the conviction that the smallest fragment torn from the edifice makes the collapse of the whole inevitable and that we must therefore defend all testimony, however debatable, by an appeal to the courts and the police, I am convinced that we would be taking a fatal path. Already in Germany there has been a public demand for the application of the penal code concerning nationalist incitement on the part of scholars who attribute to Stalin a significant part of the responsibility for the war and who speak of a "preventive war" rather than of "the German aggression against the Soviet Union." It won't be long before historians who attribute an essential role to communism in the appearance of fascism have to defend themselves before a tribunal, which could also involve the historians who "trivialize" Nazism by establishing a parallel between it and communism.

In reunified Germany there are influential currents that would not only like to accept essential parts of the defunct GDR's representation of history, with certain modifications, but also start to apply the methods used when it was instituted.

All of this is apt to raise serious concerns, and I propose that in this correspondence we discuss the contemporary intellectual situation, a present that seems constituted by a "victory of the West" and that has nevertheless spawned so many disappointments. But first of all I would like to know how you view this highly delicate question of the attitude to adopt toward revisionism and whether you could even partially agree with the ideas I have developed in this letter in a very concise and certainly too summary fashion.

Respectfully yours,
ERNST NOLTE

Berlin, September 5, 1996

7

Modern Anti-Semitism

François Furet

My Dear Colleague,

Thank you for your third letter, which adds new elements to our discussion. I will begin my response with your first point, what you call the "rational core" of anti-Semitic passion.

In the two examples you give, the "rational" element is because the Jews comprise a group of people in the modern world—should I say a people?—particularly drawn toward democratic universalism in its political and philosophical form. There are multiple reasons for this, some relatively clear, others more mysterious. It is easier to understand why the Jews enthusiastically celebrated the egalitarian emancipation of individuals than to explain their exceptional contribution to the science or literature of Europe in the last two centuries. But the fact itself is incontestable and, as such, could be the object of rational examination in its various aspects even if the historical works devoted to this subject are still relatively rare.

A Privileged Relationship

It is the fact of the privileged relationship of the Jews to democratic universalism that makes possible the understanding of the particular nature of modern anti-Semitism as opposed to medieval anti-Semitism. These two forms of hatred of the Jews are not incompatible, and their effects can be cumulative. But the older form is rooted in Christianity—in the Jewish refusal to recognize the divinity of Christ—whereas the more recent form doesn't have the same content as the Christian charge. Rather, it accuses the Jews of hiding a will to dominate the world behind the abstract universality of the world of money and the Rights of Man. The process begins with a plot against each particular nation. In both cases, the Jewish idea of divine election is turned against the Jews as a curse, and the contemporary history of Europe has shown that modern anti-Semitism has had even more disastrous effects than Christian anti-Semitism.

Up to this point, it seems to me there is no disagreement between us. I willingly agree that the anti-Semite's imaginary representation of the Jew comes not only from a historical heritage but from a group of observations on the role taken by Jews in the capitalist economy, the movements of the Left, and in the intellectual life of the democratic nations of Europe. But it is the transformation of this judgment, which can be called rational, even in the case where it deplores the state of things, into an ideology of exclusion or extermination that seems to characterize the passage from the rational to the irrational. The deviation doesn't stem from passing from the laudatory or the neutral to the pejorative. It occurs through the shift of the idea that emphasizes the role played by the Jews in modernity to a means of mobilization of the masses and to imperatives of political action. The Jews cease to be depicted or analyzed for what they are. They become the constant and active agents of a plot against the nation. They provide a scapegoat to the opponents of liberal democracy.

The Idea of the Plot

The idea of the October Revolution as the product of a plot of international Judaism is part of this type of representation. I don't deny for an instant that there were numerous Jewish militants on the first Bolshevik staff as well as in the socialist movement, especially in the countries of Eastern Europe. But this is not an observation from which one can infer, even by definition, the existence of a particular Jewish plot. The accusation belongs on a different plane from that of rational thought or historical analysis.

You write to me that in our century even good minds (without embracing the idea of a Jewish plot, which implies too much intention to be accepted without proof) analyzed capitalism and Bolshevism as two sides of the same coin, one of a modernity obsessed by productivist individualism, as opposed to the Christian or *völkisch* community. Of course I know this, but I also think that this perspective can lead to anti-Semitic ideology, with the Jew constituting the composite figure of capitalism and Bolshevism. In your country, Carl Schmitt would be a good illustration of this.[1] But I don't conclude from this that his work can be reduced to it! The distance between scholarly thought, on the one hand, and ideology, on the other, must be maintained as much as possible. In the example I am analyzing, it is very true that from a philosophical angle, capitalist democracy and the socialist critique of capitalist democracy can be seen as issuing from the same history, coming from the same stock. But Nazi anti-Semitism or the extravagant European tragedy of the twentieth century, in which Hitler was in reality the most effective accomplice of Bolshevism, can only be deduced from it by going outside the limits of rational thought. It is one of the historian's most difficult tasks to try to understand what happens in between and how the political imagination of democratic man can become, literally, insane.

What Is Nazi and What Is German?

Allow me to return to two other points in your letter that I wish to comment on.

The first concerns the character of fascism as ideology and as regime. Even though by 1965 I was an admirer of your book *Three Faces of Fascism*, I was never really convinced by your argument on Maurras as a precursor to fascism. To me, Maurras, and Action Française with him, is too positivist, too close to Auguste Comte to fall easily into this category. No doubt I would tend more than you to see fascism not as counterrevolutionary, but on the contrary as providing the European Right the support of the revolutionary idea, that is, of the radical rupture with tradition. This is the meaning of the first chapter of my book: until the arrival of fascism, "antimodern" politics finds itself in a counterrevolutionary impasse. With Mussolini it finds its attraction, its magic among the popular masses. It seems to me that in fascism there is an idea of the future, something totally lacking in the counterrevolutionary politics and ideology of the nineteenth century.

The second point I wish to discuss in what you write to me is more specifically related to German history of the twentieth century. In reading your work, I always sensed to what an extent this wounded your patriotism. I can better understand this feeling because I can share it on my side, as a Frenchman. There are many episodes in the history of France in the twentieth century that do not do honor to my country, and you cite one of the worst, which is the collaboration of the police and the Vichy government with Nazi authorities in the matter of the deportation of French Jews or those residing in France. But alas, the Hitlerian apocalypse is without precedent, and the moral condemnation of Germany since 1945 is without example in the history of nations. I easily imagine the existential ground that fed your historical work and the type of passion you put into distinguishing in the crimes of Nazi Germany what is Nazi and what is German.

I share the thesis that Hitler's personality played a fundamental role in the tragedy. Without him and without his political genius turned toward evil, everything would have been different. The historians of our era, obsessed by the determinist idea and by the sociological conception of history, often tend to misjudge what was accidental in the European tragedy in the twentieth century and the role played by several men. They don't want to see that sometimes monstrous events have small causes. However, the historian is also obliged to make allowances for what is true in the functionalist thesis, because the German war machine carried out the mission assigned by the Führer to the end. And the historian can also not avoid taking into account what German culture fostered in the way of revolutionary, nationalist, "antimodern" violence before and after the First World War. I agree that these types of ideas were widespread in Europe at the time; but it seems undeniable that Weimar Germany was its privileged laboratory, notably through its universities. If the end of Nazism had the appearance of an apocalypse in your country, whereas nothing comparable accompanied the fall of Italian fascism, it is not only for reasons related to the "total" character of the war; it is also because the Nazi dictatorship truly *uprooted* Germany from its tradition in using certain elements of this tradition to its advantage.

The Role of Antifascism

This question is independent of the question of knowing if keeping the memory of Nazi crimes alive doesn't serve to hide Soviet crimes, at least in part. On this last point I share your opinion, as you know. In fact, communist "antifascism" played the role of leading people to believe that communism was only a superior form of democracy, and its propaganda was even more powerful in the decades following the end of fascist regimes. But if this "philistine" (as Marx would say) refusal to compare fascist crimes with communist crimes saddens or exasperates you for reasons I understand, it shouldn't lead you to misread the Wehrmacht's role in the horrors committed by the

German troops in Poland or in Russia and Germany's responsibility for Nazism.

In closing, I come to your remarks on the difficulty today of working on the history of our century and in particular to your question of "revisionism" regarding the Jewish genocide.

Two Distinct Forms of Discredit

That fascism and communism do not suffer a comparable discredit is explicable first by the respective character of the two ideologies, which oppose each other in terms of the confrontation between the particular and the universal.

Once heralding the domination of the strong, a defeated fascism now reveals only its own crimes. As prophet of the emancipation of men, communism, even in its political and moral failure, benefits from the gentleness of its intentions. Circumstances also played a role in this economy of memories. The Second World War, which casts its sinister shadow over us, banned fascism from humanity, whereas the Soviets were counted among its victors. And communism disintegrated from the inside, without being defeated. Its victims were above all the people of the USSR, with Russians and Ukrainians at the top of the list, whereas Nazi Germany killed mostly outside itself, the Jews, but also the Russians, the Ukrainians, the Dutch, the French, and so on. The West showed very little compassion for the distant peoples of Eastern Europe who were victims of communism, whereas it had a concrete experience of Nazi oppression.

This leads me to the extermination of the Jews, which constitutes the culminating point of crimes committed in this century in the name of a political ideology. It doesn't excuse any of the others, not the massacre of the Kulaks at the beginning of the 1930s, nor the massive assassination of the Polish elites at Katyn and elsewhere in 1940, nor the horrors of the "Great Leap Forward" in China, or the Cambodian genocide. But what distinguishes the Jewish Holocaust among these other political manifestations of evil is perhaps two things. The first thing is that the extermination enterprise targets men, women, and children solely because they were born as they were. Thus, it is independent of any intelligible consideration drawn from struggles for power. The anti-Semitic terror lost all connection with the political sphere where it was born.

The Character of the Jewish People

The second consideration is the character of the Jewish people. In the history of humanity and especially in Europe, the people of the Bible are inseparable from both classical antiquity and from Christianity. They survive as persecuted witnesses to another promise in the Christian Middle Ages. They take part in the emergence of nations and the advent of democracy in disproportionate numbers. In martyrizing them, in trying to destroy them, the Nazis killed the civilization of Europe with the weapons of one of the most civilized peoples of Europe. We—I mean the Europeans, and not only the Germans—are not free of this misfortune, which will survive us. The forms of recollection it takes, the type of pedagogy it inspires, are not always profound and can be used for political ends. But what it expresses must be taken as an essential political sentiment of the citizens of democratic countries at this century's end. It is up to the historian, and to the intellectual, more generally, to transform it into a more informed and less partisan lesson. I admit that this is not easy, but it is necessary.

On the question that occupies the last pages of your letter, I have no remarks to offer. I am not very familiar with the literature in Europe and the United States that attempts to deny the reality of the extermination of the Jews by Nazi Germany, because the little I read gave me the feeling of being faced with authors motivated more by the old anti-Semitic passion than by a desire for knowledge. On the contrary, I share your vision of Hitler as a leader completely possessed by his hatred of the Jews and of "Judeo-Bolshevism" in particular. I also agree that the refutation of "negationist" theses (I prefer this term to "revisionist," since historical knowledge proceeds by constant "revisions" of preceding interpretations) in no way conflicts with the progress of our knowledge.[2] On the contrary, the latter requires the former. Nothing is worse than to want to block the progress of knowledge, no matter what the pretext, even with the best of intentions in the world. And it is an untenable attitude in the long run and would risk leading to opposite results from those it claims to seek. This is why I share your hostility toward legislative or authoritarian treatment of historical questions. Alas, the Holocaust is part of the history of the European twentieth century. It must be even less the object of a prior prohibition, since many of its elements remain mysterious and because historiography on the subject is only beginning.

Respectfully yours,
FRANÇOIS FURET

Paris, September 30, 1996

8

Situations

Ernst Nolte

MY DEAR COLLEAGUE,

Thank you very much for your answer to my last letter, which was much too long. You reply once again with what we in Germany customarily call a "Latin" or "French" clarity. The differences that remain between us seem to me to be only differences of accentuation. I ascribe without reserve to your assertion concerning the distinctiveness of Auschwitz compared to the gulag. For my part, I sought to distinguish between the two in opposing the notions of "social extermination" and "biological extermination," and I would like simply to add that the dividing lines are not so pronounced in reality as in the world of concepts.

I also agree with your explanation of the privilege communism enjoys in public opinion by comparison with its most vehement adversary, but in this regard I would like to raise a question: Shouldn't a movement whose intentions might be qualified as "gentle" but which nevertheless imposed itself everywhere by violence and with an enormous number of victims be judged more harshly than a party whose overall intentions can be qualified as bad?

I'm particularly delighted that in these matters you also condemn subjecting declarations, arguments, and evaluations to penal sanctions, naturally with the reservation that this doesn't include insults or violent agitations—but for these there is no need to create a special penalty.

Action Française

You ask me a question I will willingly answer. I saw "pre-fascism" in Action Française because, to me, at the beginning of the twentieth century it was the most original expression of the "counterrevolutionary" tradition. I believe that this originality was expressed in the most striking manner in Maurras's short declaration: "I am an atheist, but I am Catholic." When a politico-cultural force has recourse to unusual methods of confrontation in a difficult situation, when, for example, it has its militants take to the streets to demonstrate in uniform, the profound transformation of decisive importance has not yet occurred; this is why I consider the term "austro-fascism" illegitimate, in particular.

But when a supporter of Catholic conservatism qualifies himself as "atheist" and values his freedom of conviction to the point of refusing to renounce it even in appearance, then at the center of the counterrevolution, a revolutionary act occurs that justifies the use of this new qualifier, however unspectacular this act may appear. No doubt Joseph de Maistre knew what he wanted to say when he asserted wanting not counterrevolution but the opposite of revolution. The notion of counterrevolution immediately conceals a part of revolution, and this is particularly clear in the case of Maurras. In spite of the apparent paradox, it is even more evident in Hitler, who, precisely in his anti-Judaism, is much closer to Maurras than to Mussolini. Allow me to say another word concerning my "patriotism," which you speak of as an "existential ground." In my family, we were not *deutschnational*, and when I was a child, my first love was for the oppressed queen, Marie-Thérèse, and my first hatred was toward her enemy, the aggressive king of Prussia. It took many events for me to see myself as being led to take sides with Frederick II. He was so condemned on all sides and incurred so much reprobation as incarnating "absolute evil" that his overall image could only be grossly distorted. This is a metaphor, and you will understand what I mean by it. But regarding all that I have said that could seem generally "patriotic" and even an "exoneration of Hitler," I asked myself if I would have written the same thing if I were American, English, or French. I think I can respond in the affirmative in all cases. However, to return again to this metaphor, I did not forget for an instant that Frederick the Great had in fact undertaken a war of aggression and annexation again Marie-Thérèse.

Situation

Regarding the present, which we will discuss in conclusion, I have recently reflected not only on the situation in which we find ourselves today, but also on the meaning situations can have in general and above all in the eyes of the historian. The idea that each person is "a child of his time" is obviously a platitude, but not everyone lives at the center of the same period nor in the same situation. If I am not mistaken, the years in which you studied and began teaching were marked by a "rise of the Left," of which Jean-Paul Sartre was the most outstanding representative. When I published *Fascism in Its Time*, it passed for "leftist" because I reintroduced the generic concept of "fascism" and what went with it, that is, I relativized the theory of totalitarianism, which was dominant and almost uncontested in Germany. This is why I have often been counted among those who cleared the way for the "movement of '68." But retrospectively, I still remember very clearly that I refused to take the last step in all honesty, because I knew I was in favor of the general stance of the Federal Republic of Germany, which refused all nationalist struggle "for reunification" and trusted the long-term. The temporary acceptance of the division of the country would eventually lead to its reunification. It was a unique situation from the point of view of world history, because patience has never been a virtue of divided countries. The main thesis of the book *Three Faces of Fascism* could be formulated in the following terms: even between the two wars, Germany had been truly a part of Europe; it went astray only when it radicalized a general tendency from which it was supposed to once again find a direction to its history, by giving up a second attempt at nationalist restitution of its territory of its own accord and not just by yielding to an external pressure.

Among German historians there were no notable differences as to this assessment of things, and I could also feel supported by a consensus. But in the younger generation, precisely that of 1968, this patience was rapidly transformed into a form of impatience that negatively converted the notion of "Occidental culture" and wished to combat "Western imperialism." At the same time, the aim of this patience was abolished because "recognition of the GDR" was demanded and thus the approval of the division into two states. These young people were clearly guided by the conviction that the GDR, a socialist state, incarnated the best potentialities of Germany, in spite of some "distortions," and that in the distant future it would one day be the base on which a reunited socialist Germany would be built at the heart of a socialist Europe.

It was by chance that I was named to the Free University of Berlin exactly in the years when we passed from the first phase of the student revolution, still very fluid and marked above all by the name of Rudi Dutschke, into the second dogmatically communist and Maoist phase.[1] This is when a movement similar to the "rise of the Left" in France in the fifties and sixties appeared most clearly, although, of course, limited to students and assistants and a few rare professors. But for a very large majority of university professors, as for a large majority of the population of West Berlin, the old consensus held, and my 1983 book, *Marxismus und industrielle Revolution,* made no secret of its intention to historicize Marxism in stripping it of its claim to absolute truth. But more and more a compromise imposed itself clandestinely in the rest of the Federal Republic, even among professors and journalists, who, of course, didn't go so far as to want to identify themselves with the GDR, but who directed attention almost exclusively to "the crimes of Nazism" to the point that the once obvious theory of totalitarianism and the idea of a double form of totalitarian movements and regimes were considered not merely obsolete. Henceforth, they passed for aberrations, if not crimes.

My Theory of Totalitarianism

So to assert the duality of the German states became a moral commandment. From one day to the next, it became clear to what extent I was now in disagreement with the general consensus in the Federal Republic when my article exposing the broad outlines of the "historico-genetic" version of the theory of totalitarianism appeared in the *Frankfurter Allgemeine Zeitung* on June 6, 1986. It provoked an almost unanimous indignation, which was later called "the quarrel of the historians."[2] I, myself, did not establish a connection with the "German question," and this link was secondary for me. However, certain of my adversaries made the connection and strongly insisted on it. But when the president of the Federal Republic at the time seemed to have put a stop to the controversy by taking an official position definitively in favor of my adversaries, it didn't take more than a year for the internal collapse of the communist regime in Eastern Europe and for the "patience" evoked concerning reunification to meet an almost unhoped for happy end.[3]

Suddenly, a general consensus seemed to emerge, and with few exceptions, those who formerly had been the friends of the GDR adopted the concept of totalitarianism. To juxtapose Hitler and Stalin, even Auschwitz and the gulag, soon became a sort of commonplace. Thus the current situation was born, and all those who now felt supported by a new, more general consensus seemed to be the very ones who had refused to subscribe to the absolute truth demanded by Marxist communism when the largest and most active part of the student youth was convinced of it. But as understandable as such expectations were, they soon revealed themselves to be misleading.

The German Unification

At the beginning of 1990, here and there the idea emerged of creating a "National German Foundation" destined to finance the costs of reunification. It was hoped that large groups in the German nation would be ready to consent to substantial sacrifices. But the politicians in office refused to undertake this project, and they were right to the extent that the sum of several hundred million marks that would be necessary could not be raised by voluntary gifts. This became clear over time. But it was an unfortunate political decision in 1990 to give the impression that reunification could be financed in a certain way from the Left and by pocket change. In this way, the West Germans were deprived of the possibility of imitating their ancestors who, during the period of the wars of liberation, gave "gold for iron." They were prevented from showing, through a visible sacrifice to their liberated compatriots of the former GDR, that speeches on "the society where one must always elbow one's way" (which had indoctrinated them for forty years) were wrong. This impression was confirmed for numerous inhabitants of the former GDR when only state actions were carried out, but there were no tangible acts by the West German population itself. Of course, the claim that the GDR's industry would be bought by West German capitalism and destroyed because it represented the competition was misguided. A look at Poland and Hungary would clearly reveal that a general modernization was underway and that the standard of living of the population was getting better anyway. But the way in which former GDR industry was handed over to offers of investors from the whole world gave credence to the view that the population of the East was only the pawn of a sudden upheaval and of foreign stocks.

Yesterday's extremely authoritarian system of a planned economy was dissolved without transition or explanation and replaced by the system of business competition and the plurality of parties, which, as such, had no authoritative voice and could not even justify itself. Elsewhere, also, the West Germans arrived at the idea that "capitalism," the market system spread throughout the world that Marx and Engels declared on the point of disappearing in 1850, had developed during the decades of the Cold War well beyond what it was in 1945. Moreover, at the moment when it had no more adversaries in history, it was also losing the qualities that had made it worthy of being defended, even of being loved by the great majority, as a "liberal system" and a real democracy. Precisely to the extent that the opponents of this system could no longer offer alternatives, the discourses on its monstrosity, its character contrary to human nature, once again found a certain credit. The impression was intensified (and not only in Germany) that the real decisions—on the monetary union project and the problem of immigration, for example—were made in Brussels and in Washington under the pressure of anonymous processes, without any input whatsoever from the simple citizen (the man in the street).

How Should We Orient Ourselves from Now On?

I will stop this allusive description of the situation and resume what is of particular interest for the historian: the clear situation of the Cold War has been replaced by a sort of absence of situation that makes it extremely difficult to orient oneself. To commit oneself to a "better world" is certainly praiseworthy. But beyond what in this attitude may be banal and obvious, a commitment of this sort gets entangled in great difficulties. Wouldn't it be preferable to commit to the "battle of civilizations," in Samuel Huntington's words? Or perhaps the realistic perspective would consist in each person taking the whole world into account and demonstrating the greatest capacity to adapt to the demands of his business or businesses. Likewise, transposed into the domain of the historical discipline, all doctorates, prompted by an equal objectivity but also by an equal indifference, could deal with any theme "available" anywhere and everywhere. Shouldn't we, the elders, recognize that our work depended on certain "situations" (more than we were aware), which entailed that our work was shaped by our commitments? And wasn't this situational yoke more historical, if not more scientific—assuming that we tried hard to maintain a certain detachment while accommodating some self-criticism—than what is produced by the absence of a "situation" that characterizes the monolithic world of global economy and competition in which all things are equally accessible and, therefore, can't be examined with the same cold and impartial objectivity? Or are such reflections only typical idealistic notions that raise abstract and unreal fears while diverting us from real dangers?

In fact, I see a concrete threat appear: a totally unleashed "capitalism," dominating the entire world, lets the void it carries with it be filled by an "antifascism" that simplifies and mutilates History, just as the economic system standardizes the world. But as long as such a future can be sensed as a danger, it can be opposed. Moreover, it can be opposed not simply in favor of another concrete representation of the future, but in the name of the conviction that the awareness men can have of themselves needs historical reflection and cannot be achieved by computers nor replaced by database truisms. Thus from the absence of situation, which can never be total, a new situation could result in which significant value would be accorded the fact of assimilating History, even if historical situations no longer exist in the sense current up until now.

Please excuse me for talking so much of Germany and of myself. I would be happy if you could undertake a description of the situation in France in the postwar period from your perspective and also correlatively the situation of historiography in France, as unpleasant as is the brevity that space limitations impose on us here. I suppose our differences will emerge in as notable a manner as our proximities; indeed, even our agreements might well become visible in the end.

Respectfully yours,
ERNST NOLTE

                              Berlin, December 11, 1996

9

Such Is the Melancholy Backdrop of This Century's End

François Furet

DEAR SIR,

Thank you for your last letter. I will now take my turn in attempting to situate our respective views in relation to each other. I am, of course, more confident of success where my own views are concerned!

To the extent that the historian is prisoner of his time, and that the history he writes is also in History, we are the children of two different situations. In postwar France, when I was doing my studies, the intellectual atmosphere was dominated by the Marxist philosophy of History, for a variety of reasons. Some of these reasons were of an intellectual order but less influential than is generally thought. Marxism as a doctrinal body had no deep roots either in the intelligentsia or in the university, and the philosophical landscape of the Liberation period was dominated by Sartrian existentialism, which owed more to Heidegger

than to Marx. But much more powerful political reasons
were at work. The end of the Second World War, with the
public's discovery of Nazi crimes, seemed to put on display
a veritable tribunal of History. The Red Army was credited
with having done the lion's share of this great work of
humanity, of defeating Hitler.

Our Respective Situations

The particular circumstances of the recent history of
France added more weight to this general situation. In
May–June 1940, France was militarily crushed by Germany, and this defeat put the shameful Vichy regime in
place. This very recent past weighed heavily on the liberated country in 1944–1945. In response to this situation,
which offered good reasons to be unhappy about the recent
history of one's country, a young Frenchman of the time
could find consolation in the rise (tardy, it's true) of the
resistance movements against the Nazi occupation. But
these movements brought only two new ideas into play
in response to the bankruptcy of the Third Republic—the
Gaullist and the communist ideas.

Gaullism suffered from two drawbacks in relation to the
leftist tradition. The first was a nationalist narrowness, of
which a defeated fascism had just demonstrated the dangers, and the second was a dependency on a providential
man, something already suspect in republican ideology.
Communism, on the other hand, had the advantage of
offering a national renaissance within the context of a
democratic universalism. It offered—or seemed to offer—
both a more radical and a more modern remedy to the

decline of the nation betrayed by its elites. Through the communist idea, a young Frenchman of my generation, who had grown up in the war without having fought in it, could nourish the illusion of fulfilling the democratic ideal while working for a national renaissance. This was my case.

The situation of the young German that you were seems to me—as far as I can judge—completely different. Post-war Germany had to reflect on the national catastrophe of Nazism, which made it the object of the entire world's reprobation, but it was immunized against the attraction of the communist idea because it had just been partially conquered by the Red Army camped to the east of the country. This state of affairs left an opening for the concept of totalitarianism, which in this period, you write, enjoyed "an uncontested ascendancy" in Germany as in the United States. It is within this context that you wrote your book on "fascism in its time." If I understand you well, however, your book hesitated to draw all the conclusions of the totalitarian idea for fear of seeming to call for the reunification of Germany against the USSR. Whereas anti-communism is rejected in France for ideological reasons, it is rejected in Germany for reasons of prudence and forced moderation.

Therefore, in the beginning you and I were in very different political and intellectual situations. But this situation didn't last long, because by the mid-1950s I was part of the first diaspora of French communist intellectuals who separated themselves from communism, and in 1965 when your book appeared in French, I was one of its first admirers. This is to say that even though I don't share all the assessments (notably the analysis of Action

Française, to which I will return), I entered easily into the conceptual schema of your book, which has fascism (and Nazism) born of a double radicalization of the critique of liberalism and Marxism.

1968 and Anticommunism

But after having become comparable, our situations diverge again after the great student housecleaning of the sixties that culminated in 1968. You write that in Germany this movement ended in a condemnation of "Western imperialism" and, at the same time in a sort of rehabilitation of the GDR in the eyes of youth, to the point of seeing it as the basis of a future reunification of Germany. Thus, in your country communism would thereby tardily find the sort of immunity to criticism it enjoyed in France fifteen or twenty years before. By contrast, in France the "revolution" (I use the word for lack of a better term) of 1968 led to opposite results. It also had its Maoist current, alongside many other tendencies, some of which, for instance, hedonistic individualism, were radically "liberal." But even the Maoist current was far from being merely neo-Stalinism. It possessed libertarian anarchist nuances, as bizarre as that may seem. And it is characteristic that the work of Solzhenitsyn was received with enthusiasm in France around 1975 by many former Maoists. In other words, 1968 *also* fed anticommunism. With Solzhenitsyn, the concept of totalitarianism became established in Paris. The success of my book can be inscribed in the continuation of what began there and distinguishes the French intellectual in the European West, where the evolution of mindsets was more in line with the German example. I mean the concept of totalitarianism was progressively discredited at the moment it acquired a belated legitimacy in France.

An Atmosphere of Intolerance

It was at this time that the *unique* character of Nazism was advanced almost everywhere, not to permit a better historical understanding but, on the contrary, to forbid its analysis out of horror of the crimes it committed. If all attempts to historicize fascism (and Nazism), *a fortiori* to compare it to other contemporary experiences, are considered a culpable "understanding" in regard to these crimes, then the historians of the twentieth century might as well be silent under the threat of being accused of posthumous complicity. This atmosphere of intolerance, which is so unfavorable for intellectual work, also exists in France, notably in the press, but it is not so universal that it prevents reflection on the tragedies of our century. Here again the proof is the reception my book received even on the Left and even with the communists, who discussed it without attempting to disqualify me. On the other hand, if you were the object of a veritable trial of demonization on the part of the German Left, it seems to me it is because of two sets of reasons that differentiate your situation from mine. The first are connected to the political and "national" situation of Germany, which paradoxically makes communism a burning question at the moment of the collapse of communism, as if the totalitarian question in our century weren't the one haunting German destiny.

The others are your own, and they are at the center of our discussion. Allow me to return to them.

A German Suffering

You write to me that you don't belong to nationalism by tradition or by choice and that you would have written approximately the same things if you had been American, English, or French. On the first point, I have no reason not to believe you. Your self-analysis cannot be refuted. On the second point, however, how do you explain the fact that all your readers saw in your books the particular suffering of a German citizen struck by the tragedy of his nation and the unprecedented discredit his country fell into after the Nazi crimes? When I say all your readers, I mean not only your political adversaries in Germany, but I myself, for example, who read you with an impartial eye and also profited from doing so. Let's take your thesis, which we have already discussed, that has fascist movements arising from the Bolshevik threat. I think it is inexact to the extent that fascist ideology seems to me if not fully established, at least constituted in its principal elements before the First World War, without a link to what was then only Lenin's little party in czarist Russia. But independent of this debate, how can your insistence on the secondary or derivative character of Nazism vis-à-vis Bolshevism *not* be seen as an attempt to exonerate the former by indicting the latter? If Nazi crimes are contained in a response to Bolshevik crimes, they thereby obviously acquire a no less criminal character but a less deliberate one and, in all senses of the word, a less *primary* one.

But I would like to go a step further into the background of this commonsense statement and again raise the issue of the idea of fascism predating fascist movements. You are so well aware of the fact that a "prehistory" of fascism exists, independent of Marxism and before the First World War, that you devote the first volume of your 1965 book to it. And whom do you take as the typical representative of this prehistory? Maurras, the founder of Action Française.

The Choice of Maurras

I allow that your choice of a French writer was not deliberate on your part, even though it would have been more natural to turn toward the Italian or German political literature concerning the filiation of fascism and Nazism. I imagine that if you didn't do it, it is because, like Heidegger, you think the fascist idea is the child of Europe more than of one of the European nations in particular. This is not wrong. But the fact remains that the exceptional ravages it wrought in Germany no doubt justify the historian's focusing primarily on its German sources, which the history of ideas furnishes in abundance before the First World War and under the Weimar Republic. In the area of antiliberal thought, I don't think a richer or more radical repertory could be found.

Turning to France of the same period, for my part I accept without difficulty the demonstrations of our Israeli colleague Zeev Sternhell on the existence of a "prefascist" ideology inside French borders. But Maurras seems to me a poorly chosen example. In my eyes, as in yours, he reincarnates the French counterrevolutionary tradition at the end of the nineteenth century, the celebration of preindividual, "organic" society. But *for this very reason*, to me he is foreign to the fascist spirit, which is revolutionary, open to a fraternal society yet to be built, and not subject to a nostalgia for a hierarchical world. The model of French absolute monarchy is constantly present in Maurras, whereas all references to a past regime are nonexistent in Mussolini or Hitler (or even in Marinetti, or in the Jünger of the beginning of the 1930s). One could support the argument by a study of the respective philosophies: the philosophies of fascism are founded on the assertion of the irrational powers of life, that of Maurras is comprised of positivist rationalism drawn from Auguste Comte.

You write to me that in your eyes what allows Maurras to be classed among the pre- or parafascist thinkers is his attitude toward Catholicism: he celebrates the Catholic Church without being a believer. He likes the church as a body, as a social organ, as an image of the spiritual unity of the French. But he cannot believe what he teaches, not because, as you say, he values his "freedom of conscience," but because, as a rationalist, he cannot bend his spirit to a set of irrational beliefs. This attitude is not particular to him alone among the French of the nineteenth century. Napoleon held it before him in signing the Concordat, and after 1848 the Voltairian bourgeoisie widely shared this state of mind. The use of the church for political and social ends is a trap into which even real Catholics fall. And what is there to say, then, of others . . .

In effect, Action Française's elevation of the Catholic Church to the status of the spiritual power of the nation, even though the founders of the doctrine didn't believe in Catholicism's dogmas, is a central contradiction of Action

Française, and this contradiction finally ruined the movement after its condemnation by Rome.[1] But I don't see in
what way this contradiction is original or "revolutionary."

Fascism Is Revolutionary

With this last adjective, perhaps I touch on what separates our conceptions of fascism. For me, the novelty
of fascism in History consists in its emancipation of the
European Right from the impasse that is inseparable from
the counterrevolutionary idea. In effect, in the nineteenth
century the counterrevolutionary idea never ceased being
trapped in the contradiction of having to use revolutionary
means to win without being able to assign itself any goal
other than the restoration of a past from which, however,
the revolutionary evil arose. There is nothing like this in
fascism. It is no longer defined by a *re-action* (reversal)
against a revolution. It is itself the revolution. I think
that by insisting on underscoring the reactive character
of fascism, you underestimate its novelty. After all, what
needs to be understood is the formidable attraction it
held for the masses of the twentieth century, whereas the
counterrevolutionary idea had none of this influence in
the preceding century.

Melancholy

You end your letter with questions about the present that
I share. You very rightly note that the collapse of Soviet communism was curiously accompanied in Europe

by a move of public opinion toward the Left. The more capitalism triumphs, the more it is despised. With the Soviet Union it has lost one of its foils, which had made it the showcase of freedom. It has been deprived of its best argument—anticommunism. The critique of its misdeeds is freer, more open, easier now that it is free from the obligation of celebrating a police socialism. What is curious about it is that the European Left is not held responsible for either its accommodation or its support of this police socialism. Since it only uses the socialist idea negatively now as a critique of capitalism and no longer as support for an existing regime, it has again found a less vulnerable discourse. It no longer has to justify another society, because no other society exists anymore. It can be content to criticize democratic society as nondemocratic, that is, incapable of answering the expectations it created and the promises it made. It is now rooted only in the oldest dream of modern democracy, which consists of separating democracy and capitalism, to keep one and drive out the other, when together they form a single history.

Such is the melancholy backdrop of this century's end. Here we are enclosed in a single horizon of history, pulled toward the standardization of the world and the alienation of the individual from the economy, condemned to slow the effects without having a hold on their causes. History appears all the more sovereign as we lose the illusion of governing it. But as always, the historian must react against what seems inevitable at the time he writes; he knows too well that these kinds of collective givens are ephemeral. The forces that work toward the universalization of the world are so powerful that they trigger sequences of events and situations incompatible with the idea of the laws of history, *a fortiori* of possible prediction. Understanding and explaining the past is already difficult enough.

With deepest respect,
FRANÇOIS FURET

Paris, January 5, 1997

Notes

All notes have been provided by the series editor, Richard Golsan, unless otherwise specified.

Preface

1. The term *negationist* is borrowed from the French word *négationnisme*, denial of the Holocaust. *Trans.*

Foreword

1. *The Passing of an Illusion.* Trans. Deborah Furet (Chicago: U of Chicago P, 1999). English titles will be used in the text where available; however, this title will appear in French since page references cited are to the French edition. *Trans.*

1. On Nolte's Interpretation of Fascism

1. This text by François Furet is excerpted from his last book, *Le Passé d'une illusion: Essai sur l'idée communiste au XX siècle* (Paris: Laffont and Calmann-Lévy, 1995), pp. 194–96. *Ed., French ed.*

2. Mussolini, of course, began his political career as a socialist and was editor for many years of the party newspaper *Avanti!* before elaborating the fascist doctrine and becoming the movement's leader in the aftermath of World War I. For a detailed account of Mussolini's political evolution see Dennis Mack Smith, *Mussolini: A Biography* (New York: Vintage Books, 1982).

3. For an excellent discussion of the Historians' Debate in English, see Charles S. Maier, *The Unmasterable Past: History, the Holocaust, and German National Identity* (Cambridge: Harvard UP, 1988). The original documents of the debate are published in English translation in *Forever in the Shadow of Hitler? Original Documents of the Historikerstreit, the Controversy Concerning the Singularity of the Holocaust.* Trans. James Knowlton and Truett Cates (Atlantic Highlands N.J.: Humanities Press, 1993).

4. "Negationist" is the term used most often in France for someone who denies that the Holocaust occurred. The term was first coined by Henry Rousso in *The Vichy Syndrome* (Cambridge: Harvard UP, 1991) in his discussion of the Faurisson Affair. See Rousso, pp. 151–57.

5. Cf. Hans Christof Kraus, "L'historiographie philosophique d'Ernst Nolte," in *La Pensée politique*, Hautes Etudes-Le Seuil-Gallimard, 1994, pp. 59–87; Alain Renaut, preface to Ernst Nolte, *Les Mouvements fascistes*, 2nd edition, coll. Liberté de l'esprit directed by Raymond Aron, 1991, pp. 6–24 (Paris: Calmann-Lévy). *Author, French ed.*

2. Beyond Ideological Impasses

1. In its 1996 issue (no. 89), *Le Débat* invited a number of distinguished historians, including Renzo de Felice, Eric Hobsbawm, Robert Conquest, and Nolte himself, to respond to *The Passing of an Illusion* and assess its impact on discussions of the history and nature of communism, the meaning of totalitarianism, and the comparison of communism with fascism. Nolte's essay (pp. 139–46) is titled "Sur la théorie du totalitarisme."

2. In *The Passing of an Illusion,* Furet discusses the impact of the revolutionary tradition in France on the intellectual Left's reception of the Russian Revolution. He has also, of course, written numerous other texts on the comparison of the two revolutions and their respective receptions (and the interpretations of these receptions) in France.

3. François-Victor-Alphonse Aulard was a late nineteenth–

early twentieth century historian of the French Revolution known for his positivist approach. He was the first full professor of revolutionary history at the Sorbonne. His contemporary, Albert Mathiez, known for the intensity of his archival research, was more socialistic in outlook, influenced by thinkers like Jean Jaurès and Lenin. Both figures are discussed and criticized by Furet in *Critical Dictionary of the French Revolution* (Cambridge: Harvard UP, 1989) in the chapter titled "The Academic History of the Revolution."

4. François Furet left the Communist Party in the mid- to late 1950s, although there is disagreement as to the actual date. The possible dates range from 1954 to 1959.

5. Nolte is referring here to Furet's article "Entre Israël et la gauche française: trente ans de malentendus," which originally appeared in *Nouvel Observateur* on May 13, 1978. The article has been reprinted in François Furet, *Un Itinéraire intellectuel. L'historien-jounaliste, de "France-Observateur" au "Nouvel Observateur," 1958–1977* (Paris: Calmann-Lévy, 1999), pp. 460–64.

3. A Taboo Subject

1. The Popular Front coalition, consisting of Socialists, Communists, and Radicals, took power in June 1936 under the premiership of the Socialist Léon Blum. The Popular Front came about largely in reaction to a perceived fascist threat in France, especially in the wake of the right wing–inspired riots of February 6, 1934.

2. See Hannah Arendt, *The Origins of Totalitarianism* (New York: Harvest/HBJ Books, 1979).

4. From the Gulag to Auschwitz

1. François Furet, "Sur l'illusion communiste," *Le Débat*, no. 89, March–April 1996, p. 170 ff. *Ed., French ed.*

2. "Weil man die Juden nicht als Mitwirkende in einer Tragödie, sondern nur [!] als Opfer in einem Schurkenstreich sehen will." *Author, French ed.*

3. "Tsiganes" and "romanichels." *Trans.*

6. On Revisionism

1. In English in the original. *Trans.*

2. Count Joseph Arthur Gobineau, racial theorist and author of *Essai sur l'inégalité des races humaines* (1853), had considerable influence on subsequent racist doctrines, especially in Germany. Theodor Fritsch was a Leipzig engineer and the author of anti-Semitic tracts including *Handbook of the Jewish Question* and *Anti-Semitic Catechism*, both of which enjoyed numerous editions. Beginning in 1902, Fritsch published a journal, *Der Hammer*, which extolled racial purity. Heinrich von Treitschke was a respected German historian at Berlin University in the late nineteenth century. His endorsement of anti-Semitism—he was known for statements such as "the Jews are our misfortune"—gave anti-Semitism an aura of respectability that it had not previously enjoyed.

3. It is important to note that the French police did "participate with alacrity" in the deportations of foreign *and* French Jews as of summer 1942 in accordance with arrangements made along these lines between German officials and the head of Vichy police, René Bousquet. The deportations have, moreover, been reported in the press in France for many years and not just by the press of the "radical Left" as Nolte suggests.

4. Paul Rassinier (1906–1967) was a pacifist and official of the French Socialist Party (SFIO) before World War II. Involved in the Resistance, Rassinier was arrested and deported to the Dora concentration camp. After the war, Rassinier became increasingly outspoken first in downplaying and then denying the Holocaust in works including *Le Mensonge d'Ulysse* (1961).

5. Nolte is referring here to theses developed in Gar Alperovitz's *Atomic Diplomacy: Hiroshima and Potsdam* (London: Pluto Press, 1994), originally published in the United States in 1975. According to the introduction of the 1985 edition, the book argued that possession of the atomic bomb served as a "master card" in United States diplomatic relations with the

Soviet Union even before it was dropped on Hiroshima and Nagasaki, and that a major reason the bomb was used was "to make the Soviet Union more manageable" (1). Alperovitz's thesis has apparently gained wider acceptance in recent years, and it does challenge the notion that the Soviet Union was solely responsible for the "East-West conflict" to which Nolte refers. It is not clear, however, that Alperovitz was arguing that the "first atomic bomb targeted Japan less than the Soviet Union," as Nolte contends in his letter to Furet.

7. Modern Anti-Semitism

1. Carl Schmitt, author of *The Concept of the Political* (1927) and many other works, was a distinguished legal and political philosopher before the war and a supporter of Nazism and its policies. For an excellent discussion of Schmitt, his views, and their influence, see "Carl Schmitt, Political Existentialism, and the Total State," in Richard Wolin, *The Terms of Cultural Criticism: The Frankfurt School, Existentialism, Poststructuralism* (New York: Columbia UP, 1992) pp. 83–104.

2. For the opposite view—that one should not attempt to refute negationist theses because de facto this gives them a certain intellectual legitimacy—see Pierre Vidal Naquet, *Assassins of Memory: Essays on the Denial of the Holocaust* (New York: Columbia UP, 1992).

8. Situations

1. Rudi Dutschke was the leader of the student protest movements in West Germany in the late 1960s.

2. Nolte is here referring to the article, "A Past That Will Not Pass Away." It is important to stress that Nolte's essay alone did not precipitate the Historians' Debate, as he seems to imply. The publication of Andreas Hillgruber's *Two Kinds of Destruction*, which at least implicitly compared the Holocaust to German suffering at the hands of the invading Red Army at the end of the war, also stirred considerable controversy.

3. According to Jeffrey Herf, in October 1988, Richard von Weizsäcker "criticized those who compared or equated Auschwitz with the Gulag and other cases of ruthless extermination." Weizsäcker stated: "Auschwitz remains unique. It was perpetrated by Germans in the name of Germany." See Herf, *Divided Memory: The Nazi Past in the Two Germanys* (Cambridge: Harvard UP, 1997), p. 359.

9. Such Is the Melancholy Backdrop

1. Action Française was banned by the Pope in 1926 for "putting the interests of parties ahead of those of religion and making the latter serve the interests of the former."

IN THE EUROPEAN HORIZONS SERIES

The Consecration of the Writer, 1750–1830
By Paul Bénichou
Translated and with an introduction by Mark Jensen
With a preface by Tzvetan Todorov

*A Modern Maistre: The Social and Political Thought of
Joseph de Maistre*
By Owen Bradley

Dispatches from the Balkan War and Other Writings
By Alain Finkielkraut
Translated by Peter S. Rogers and Richard Golsan
With an introduction by Richard Golsan

Fascism and Communism
By François Furet and Ernst Nolte
Translated by Katherine Golsan
With a preface by Tzvetan Todorov

Stalinism and Nazism: History and Memory Compared
Edited by Henry Rousso
English-language edition edited and introduced by
Richard J. Golsan
Translated by Lucy B. Golsan, Thomas C. Hilde, and
Peter S. Rogers

A Primer of Italian Fascism
Edited and with an introduction by Jeffrey Schnapp
Translated by Jeffrey T. Schnapp, Olivia E. Sears,
and Maria G. Stampino

Politics and Guilt: The Destructive Power of Silence
By Gesine Schwan
Translated by Thomas Dunlap

Life in Common: An Essay in General Anthropology
By Tzvetan Todorov
Translated by Katherine Golsan and Lucy Golsan
With a new afterword by the author

Lightning Source UK Ltd.
Milton Keynes UK
UKOW06f2345200116

266802UK00019B/154/P